NARCISSISTIC
FATHERS

A Practical Guide for Adult Children to Deal
with Emotional Abusive Toxic Fathers and
Recover from CPTSD

(Complex Post-Traumatic Stress Disorder)

Rose Mary Parker

Narcissistic Fathers

Narcissistic Fathers

Narcissistic Fathers

TABLE OF CONTENT

INTRODUCTION

Are you wondering why your father made your childhood so miserable? Do you sometimes rack your brain on why your father seems so different?

In the family with a perverse narcissistic father, there is only one very bright star: him. "Dark" sun of the family, the partner and the children exist only as satellite planets that orbit around it, reflecting their light.

The children, born to become the extension of the perverse narcissist, can have different functions: allow parents to brag about his family:

"look what beautiful children I have generated," or guarantee him a socially desirable image.

The perverse narcissist father always changes personality and behavior outside his home. He can transform himself into the opposite of what appears at home. People are only an audience to which to show the best part of themselves; therefore, in front of them will wear the mask of the "best father, "impeccable, smiling, caring to the needs of children, and always ready to sacrifice for them.

This only increases the family drama of these children, forced not only to bear daily harassment but even unable to find understanding and comfort in the people they have close to them. Out of the family, people are unaware of the true nature of the narcissist and, therefore, too often, they are ready to defend him. Young children are brought to act as their parents to demonstrate to the spectators in the audience that he/she has received an excellent education from a charming, perfect, and brilliant father, able to raise beautiful children and above the average.

However, if on the one hand, a perverse narcissistic father wants his children to reflect his grandeur, on the other hand, he scares about the comparison. This happens especially when the children are becoming young adults, revealing the fundamental needs of autonomy and identification, choosing a university or professional career that he doesn't approve, as he feels threatened by them. The Narcissistic father only crushes his children, through fierce denigrations and devaluations, to avoid to obscure his grandiose image and so that he can continue undisturbed to be the despotic king of his family.

Narcissistic fathers and mothers love to sow weeds among their children, placing them against each other while they, from the small throne where they sit, watch them destroy themselves, without getting their hands dirty.

Children are challenged continuously through constant comparison. Generally, he elects a "golden child" and a "scapegoat child."

The first is the idealized extension of the father, or "the chosen one," the one who is destined for great awards and honors, as desired by the narcissistic father for himself. Everything is allowed to him/her. Family lives revolve (at least apparently) around his needs, his will, and his whims. This son gets the semblance of being loved and, in return, sacrifices himself on the altar of his narcissistic father, believing he is truly worthy of love and accepted for this to put his life at his service. Not infrequently, this child has to task to take care directly of the parent's narcissistic, psychologically, or physically abusing the scapegoat, to relieve the narcissistic father from this task.

The scapegoat child's function is to be the container for the garbage that the narcissistic parent cannot accept to keep. On him are continually deposited all the parts that the narcissus father cannot accept to have. This child will be incapable, ugly, the least intelligent, brilliant, or creative, the one too introverted or inadequately extroverted, dull, inadequate, awkward, the "wild child" of the family — someone to be ashamed of, someone to isolate and deny as soon as possible. The scapegoat is the bearer of that "defect" on alters of perfection of the narcissistic parent and the family.

Whether they are golden children or scapegoats, they are sadly alone because children of a narcissistic family cannot ally with the healthy parent, as in these family's rules:

"If one parent is a perverse narcissist, the other is dominated by it."

The children thus grow up alone, suffering in silence and watch, often powerless, the succubus parent bend to the will of the perverse one. This also happens when the succubus parent has qualities that could guarantee an emotionally healthy growth of the children because the satisfaction of the needs of the perverse partner takes away the clarity and the necessary energy to take care of the children. The obstinate narcissistic father succeeds in his plan by manipulating, mystifying, subjecting his wife to gaslighting or defamatory campaigns, and continually devaluing her in front of her children.

"In front of the world, the relationship with my father is perfect, but behind closed doors, everything changes."

This behavior will teach, especially to the son, that devaluing and minimizing the merits of the mother, sister, and all the women he will know in his life, is normal.

Frequently, the narcissistic fathers harm sons more than daughters: this is because the father sees in the child and young man an extension of himself, rather than an independent person, with his dreams, desires, psychological and physical issues to be implemented.

In this arid family scenario, what can be the psychopathological outcomes for the children?

Typically, the son of the narcissistic family is animated by a blind rage that can act openly or passively-aggressively. Overwhelming feelings of emptiness often overcome. He feels inadequate and incapable. It can also have severe episodes of anxiety and depression or manifest significant psychosomatic disorders.

The identification process for the son is always difficult: the father proposes an unacceptable male model, and it is not uncommon for the son of narcissistic fathers to develop problems related to gender identity.

The perverted narcissistic parents never identify in themselves any responsibility for any mental disorders manifested by their children.

During a session with a narcissistic father, I received a typical narcissistic answer:

"I have been an exemplary father. This guy is a disaster for our family. With his behavior, he throws mud on my respectable family. We are hard workers, honest people like my parents and all my ancestors ".

I didn't find any introspective and self-criticism ability on him. He gave all responsibility for his son's suffering to the bad companies, the consumer society, and the values of the past that they are no longer there.

Only God knows if he would not have accused even the aliens of having kidnapped and corrupted her forever, to avoid to recognize that he had generated part of that pain on her.

Being exposed from childhood to such psychological abuse generates a colossal confusion that damages the emotional life of the children. He would be torn from the desire to disown the abusive father and the sense of guilt "because, in any case, he is always my father and also he, like everyone else, has a good side. "

This is one of the perverse dynamics that leads many daughters of narcissistic fathers to see in the obstinate narcissistic partners something familiar that makes them, somehow, "feel at home." Following this behavior, they would not recognize and identify the abuse they suffer. It is not an easy task sometimes because sometimes we are not so brave to see over the curtain. But if you decide to lift the curtain on Narcissistic Father Abuse, you can never go back to the way things were. We must be an actor and spectators of the drama to understand human beings.

I can not guarantee that you will definitely recover from the deep wounds inflicted by your Narcissistic Father. Still, I can promise that this will an essential step in your journey for healing and happiness.

It is not an easy task sometimes because we are not so brave to see over the curtain.

Thank you for choosing Narcissistic Fathers. I hope you will find useful information about your awareness and life changing. I would appreciate hearing your thoughts with a short review on Amazon.

Narcissistic Fathers

PART ONE: NARCISSISM[1]

Chapter 1: Origin of Narcissism

Narcissism is a term that was coined by Paul Nacke in 1899 to refer to someone that was treated as an object. This term was taken up by Freud, and he went ahead to bring up more information about it.

Since this time, the concept of narcissism has grown over borders, and thoughts and theories have come up to make it part of our daily lives.

Note [1]: PART ONE of this book is taken from *"Narcissistic Mothers: A practical guide for Daughter and Son to Recognize a Narcissistic Parent Abuse and How to Heal and Recover from CPTSD"*, adapting the text on the subject of this book.

Many people use the word to refer to personal vanity – the desire to make ourselves look better than anyone else.

Just like any other personality disorder, this condition shows a never-ending pattern of behavior that affects the social, professional, and familial relationships of the one suffering from it. These people have an inflated opinion of their perceived abilities or traits. Narcissism makes people feel even more egoistic as they gain the Admiration and praise of other people. Many of them often show that they are superior, but others know how to hide it under acts of pretentious humility. But this is usually ruined when they get criticized. They typically respond by showing rage or making condescending remarks toward the person who offended them with criticism.

People who are suffering from narcissistic personality disorder show sure signs of selfishness; They don't know the meaning of empathy, although some of them may pretend to show it. Some narcissists who have become experts at hiding their disorder may look like they are very generous, understanding, and selfless. But this behavior usually doesn't last.

Narcissism usually develops in early childhood. It seems the emotional trauma responsible for narcissism occurs around the age of a toddler. Hence the narcissist's ability to handle emotions gets stuck at that level of mental development. That explains their dangerous emotional immaturity, doesn't it?

We all get exposed to trauma during the early stages of our development. It's only inevitable. Injury can result from something as simple as not being picked up by our parent as a baby or being fed against our will. It could also result from something more severe, as our mother left us at the kindergarten for the first time, which can cause a long-lasting fear of separation. Our parents fighting and screaming at each other in our presence can leave their imprints on our subconscious mind, too. So, what kind of trauma produces a narcissist?

Growing up with an either overbearing and completely neglectful parent can warp a child's mind and cause them to be narcissistic adults later in life. A parent can be overbearing when it comes to a child's performance in school and neglectful when it comes to a child's emotional needs.

The trauma of a narcissist is the perceived lack of control. The inability to acknowledge their own emotions makes a narcissist extremely uncomfortable. Admitting one "wrong" thing about themselves would make them feel as though everything is wrong. So, every abusive and manipulative action they take only serves one purpose: to feel in control. The root of their toxic behavior towards you has nothing to with you, and it has everything to do with them. If you play close attention to their accusations, you will see that they, in fact, project their behavior, fears, and doubts on you. A narcissist may often lie, yet accuse you of lying all the time, no matter how much proof you present that they are wrong.

You must keep in mind that narcissists never truly learned how to express and process their emotions. Their parents may have been overly protective and proud of them – but only when they fulfilled their parents' expectations. One could try to do some research about the past of the narcissist in question. Though it usually is challenging to get a clear picture. It's complicated to find the truth about a narcissist, especially when their parents admit to not having been able to handle their child.

In many cases, one or both of their parents may display some narcissistic traits, too. That does not mean, however, that the children of a narcissist are bound to become narcissistic as well.

This can be an environmental cause that can lead to a forced image of perfection later in life. Another aspect is early childhood abuse. One way to deal with abuse is to see yourself as above it, too clean for it. Taking an abusive history into account, narcissism acts as a wall to prevent being hurt further in the future. Despite the several ways the disorder can be environmental, there is also some belief that the trait can, in fact, be hereditary. With genetics, though, seeing a specific behavioral feature can be difficult. Often, though it may seem genetic, it is moreover the way that parent or grandparent was raised that gives them the condition. This brings up the question of actual genetics. Science has yet to come to a clear conclusion on that, though. Studies have not been able to go to a solid end, and with many different conditions, it is hard to see which is environmental and which is genetic.

The majority of the cases of Narcissistic Personality Disorder, though, always points back to the parents who raised the child. Whether it is neglect, abuse, overprotection, rewarding for insignificance, Munchausen, or even the parent giving the child a hypochondriac disorder or a sense that they are superior, the child's behavior is usually created at an early age. With such a deep-seated basis and such a long time for growth, this makes the disorder even harder to overcome later in life. Changing someone's perspective of how they should see the world when they were raised and to see it differently can be a nearly impossible task. This also can cause more behavioral and personality issues. Taking away the one or only defense someone has constructed to deal with trauma can then lead to an exposed and vulnerable feeling that can cause depression and anxiety. What happens then is the person goes from being narcissistic to high-risk Avoidant Personality Disorder, agoraphobia, social anxiety, self-harm, and even suicidal, or an intention of hurting others. People using narcissism to cover an abusive or traumatic childhood would have to be approached with the utmost care.

Even if the issues are genetic, there is really no direct way to treat genetics over a learned behavior cycle. Hereditary behavior issues are something a species line has evolved to. Somehow that series of genetics has evolved into seeing itself as more significant than others. Whether this has to do with the biological mating habits or some kind of protective reaction of the line, it is part of who the person is. Just as someone is likely to have a stronger inclination to be a leader or one who helps people for a living, being someone who sees themselves as above others will already be in their head from early childhood. As with learned behavior, this comes from one or both parents. If the parent(s) has the same genetic disposition, then they will raise the child with that frame of mind, once again, the person is locked in a cycle. Being both genetically superior and raised to believe that they are so will be the prime persona of the person and thus something which is not easy to change.

Notes:

_____

_____

_____

_____

_____

_____

_____

_____

_____

_____

_____

_____

_____

_____

_____

_____

_____

_____

_____

_____

_____

_____

_____

_____

_____

_____

_____

_____

Narcissistic Fathers

Narcissistic Fathers

Chapter 2: Identifying a Narcissist

You know that work colleague or friend who always manages to be at the center of attention, making everything to be about them. What about that family member who is in the habit of demeaning everyone because they believe they are smarter than everybody else?

Interacting with a narcissist can be daunting, and that's why it is essential to be able to identify their dominating character traits. The truth is that they are no physical body tests that one can perform to ascertain the presence of narcissism. But it is possible to observe certain behavior and reactions and identify this condition.

An inflated sense of self-importance

They believe that they are exceptional and unusual and can only interact with others "unique." In other words, they are too good for anything ordinary or average and only want to associate with other high-ranking people, places or things

They will exaggerate their achievements and capabilities and make everyone feel how lucky they are to have them in their lives. They are the undisputed heroes, and everyone else ranks second in their hierarchy.

A sense of entitlement and preeminence

Because of their overestimated sense of importance, narcissists expect favorable treatment whenever they go. They consider themselves unique and believe that they should get everything they want. They expect everyone around them to be at their beck and call and comply with their every wish and whim. If you don't comply and meet their every need, then the term you as useless.

Unrealistic need for praise and Admiration

Narcissists' sense of grandiose is like a balloon that needs a constant supply of air to keep it inflated. Likewise, their ego requires a steady source of applause and validation to keep it inflated. The occasional compliment does not count, and that's why they surround themselves with people who are willing to feed their ego with words of affirmation and praise continually.

These interactions are one-sided as it is always about what the devotee can do to the narcissist and not the other way round. And if there is ever a breach or a reduction of praise and affirmation from the admirer, the narcissist treats that as disloyalty, and the devotee will face dire consequences.

Lives in a perfect world that supports their delusions

Narcissists will dwell in this fantasy bubble, and anything that threatens to burst it is met with extreme range and defensiveness. Facts and opinions that intimidate them are ignored or rationalized, and so those around the narcissist must learn to trend carefully for peace to prevail. They have a warped sense of perception about things around them.

Lack of empathy for other people

Narcissists are not able to identify with the feelings of other people. In other words, they cannot put themselves in other people's shoes but exploit without guilt or shame. To them, the people around them are there to serve their needs and replenish their insatiable thirst for approval.

To that end, they don't think twice about taking advantage of others to achieve their desires. In most cases, this exploitation is glaring, and in these others, it is subtle and hard to be noticed.

Narcissisms don't consider how their manipulative behaviors affect others, and even if you try to point out to them, they simply don't get it. All they think about is how to satisfy their needs and feed their egos.

Meticulousness

Many narcissists have an extremely high sense of perfection. They believe that things should happen exactly as planned, and life should be as they envision it in their minds. This is an impossible demand in the real world, which results in the narcissist feeling miserable and depressed all the time.

Narcissists who are inclined to perfection are very difficult to please. Nothing you do will be right enough, and you are always to meet their infinite needs for Admiration, love, service, or purchases. Failure to meet these desires may lead to dismissal. They cannot take a "no" and often expect others to inconvenience themselves so that they can serve them.

They want to be in control

We have established that most narcissists are perfectionists, and when they feel things are not working out to their stands, they develop this great need to controlling other words. They will do anything possible to be in control of a situation and manipulate it to their liking.

With their unreasonably high sense of entitlement, they will demand to control events because they believe it is the logical thing to do. In essence, they have everything figured out in their minds. They have a storyline in mind and have assigned specific roles to each person in that particular set up. If any person behaves contrary, the narcissist becomes very agitated because you have unsettled what was in the script. You are a threat to their desired outcome.

Thrive in the blame game

In most cases, the narcissist will blame the one person who is the most loyal and emotionally attached to them. This dedicated admirer is the safest to blame because the chances of denying or rejecting the blame are very minimal.

Thrill-seekers

Anyone working with a narcissist will find themselves in a roller coaster, swinging in random directions. You will conform to the activity that brings the maximum thrill to the narcissist. When the adrenaline rush hits, strategic plans are thrown out of the window and replaced by reactivity to a self-inflicted crisis. The bottom line is that narcissist is forever chasing thrill because the resulting excitement makes them feel good about themselves. The excitement also serves as an outlet for all the pressure and aggression that is usually bottled up in them.

Extreme sensitivity to criticism

They will attack and hurl all manner of insults to their critics and banish them from their perceived glorious presence. Narcissists will expect their opponents to be devastated when not in their coverage, and this gives them a sense of pride and importance.

Surprisingly, the same people who dread to be criticized are overly critical of other people. They can see their own problems but believe other people are problematic and need to change.

Lack of a sense of humor

Narcissists are too severe in their life. They don't get jokes, and they don't make jokes except for a few sarcastic remarks and weird puns. Their lack of empathy makes them not to grasp the context and emotional aspects of the words, actions, jokes, and humor expressed. For a person to laugh at a joke or make a humorous relevant, he/she must, first of all, understand the context and effect of the people around him. Narcissists lack this critical concept and consequently specialize in sarcasm, which they mistake for wits.

Have undefined interpersonal boundaries

Narcissists will unconsciously view others as extensions of themselves. They can't tell where they end and where the other person begins. They regard other people as existing solely to serve them and will disregard their needs, family obligations, and any other duty that their loyal followers have to fulfill. They are regarded as 'narcissists supply,' existing mainly to cater to their personal needs, and therefore it is difficult for the narcissist to think of them indecently. They generally expect their devotees to be at their beck and call.

Notes:

_____

_____

_____

_____

_____

_____

_____

_____

_____

_____

_____

_____

_____

_____

_____

_____

_____

_____

_____

_____

_____

_____

_____

_____

_____

_____

_____

Narcissistic Fathers

Chapter 3: What is narcissism?

Narcissism is when you love yourself way more than others. These kinds of individuals give priority to their desires and needs over anyone else's. They care about nobody except themselves. People who showcase this behavior are known as narcissists.

You can notice narcissism in different kinds of individuals, including coworkers, spouses, family members, and friends. The boss who always undermines you at work regardless of what you do can be a narcissist. It could also be your parent who makes you feel less for refusing to do their bidding.

Narcissists can also channel most of their efforts into being the best they can be in the eyes of the public. They thrive on attention and enjoy it when others are envious of them, even though they exhibit unhealthy behaviors to people they live with.

They are charming enough to attract people to like them, to make them think that they are amazing. It is common for them to make prospects fall in love so they can be their true narcissistic selves without the risk of being abandoned.

Narcissism is a character trait in which someone displays a heightened over-confidence due to their Admiration of themselves; they can simply do no wrong. This is an exaggerated behavior that breathes and exudes arrogance, pretentiousness, and a deep-rooted ideology of false superiority. "I am special. Everyone else in the world is below me because they are not me". A person who exhibits narcissistic characteristics is often described as being cocky, self-centered, self-absorbed, and rude. They view life as a playground for manipulating emotion, as an untapped market in which to exploit and to bend the truth at will. They can be considered to be "winners," but they are crude people to be involved with due to their self-described perfection. So, too, are they, liars. Their success — in most cases — is because of their total and complete disregard for other people and their feelings. Or rather, narcissists will push past people no matter what those people are feeling. They view other people as obstacles. We are their next hurdle to get over. They would most likely push us off the edge of a top-floor balcony if it meant that they would get just a little more ahead of everyone else.

Narcissists are the perennial interrupters of conversation. They continuously crave the limelight; they feel as if they deserve everyone's attention at every single turn. They want to be seen. They want to be heard. They want to be the leading figure in any small gathering, work circles, friendship circles, and among the large crowds. They are the people who ooze confidence in every moment. They are very charming people, and more often than not, they are quite funny, very sarcastic. They are an excellent company in public. Still, once at home and in their respective comfort zones, they shed their beautiful skins for the emotionally deprived, ostentatious colors that they don't have when returned to their private and intimate places. They use manipulation and excessive, yet believable, lies as a tool to such an extent that narcissists are almost fanatical individuals regarding their use of such methods.

Narcissists have such a deep self-belief burning within them. But beneath all of that lies a person who has been deeply affected by life. Narcissists are people, though pretty hardcore ones, who have been shaped by past trauma, past experiences, or past abuse. Narcissism has crafted them into a person with such anxiety that the line between nervousness and abandonment has morphed and blurred into a singularly individualistic focus. The Admiration that they are continually seeking is due to their inner mental conflicts that were borne from a lonely and possibly unloved childhood. This has made them develop what we could call external spotlighted arrogance. The definition of this is, simply, a spotlight. Some form of the inner spotlight that externalizes itself – or switches on - when it feels like it needs to be seen, it burns so bright that it forces people to shift and focus all undivided attention on the narcissist. This trait, or behavioral characteristic, if looked at from a psychological perspective, is most common in children below the age of 10. It is that you need to stand out from the rest, to get attention, whether that is from your parents, your family, your friends. It's a phase our brains go through during early childhood development that can be best linked to the behavior-type of somebody that wants to brag about something. In a narcissist's case, what they are mostly bragging about is themselves.

We all know a narcissist. They could be our mother or our father; they could have been this way for as long as we can remember and have left us, now in adulthood, shattered, confused, exhausted. They could be our brother or our sister. They were always showered with praise, always told that they were the star – they were serial winners and developed an egotism that has become the prospective difficulties in our lives, still affecting us at this very moment. They could be a work colleague or employee. But what are the roots of narcissism?

Narcissists tend to view themselves quite differently when compared to others, and they often make those around them feel inadequate and devalued. Here's the kicker—a narcissist always wants everything to be about themselves. You might not mind showering a one-year-old infant with all your attention, but you will start to mind when a 35-year-old demands the same level of care and achieves it at your expense.

Narcissists easily victimize others by just being who they are, and it is unlikely they will ever change. This might seem rather severe, but until you deal with a narcissist, you will not realize how toxic, such individuals can be. To understand NPD, you must first understand the way narcissists think about themselves.

Narcissists are often characterized by high self-worth. This characteristic affects the thoughts and behaviors of an individual, as well as his interaction with others.

Narcissism is considered normal up to a certain extent. When it gets to the extreme, it turns into a disorder (NPD). A person that is full of himself, and one finds it difficult to appreciate others, can be considered as a narcissist. Narcissism is also evident in individuals who love too much attention and those who exercise a high sense of superiority. Some people call it self-centeredness or self-love.

It is always easy to identify a narcissistic person in a group of people. Such individuals always hype the crowd and keep sharing stories about themselves. They always seem to be more interested in their success. Narcissists tend to be manipulated and often lack a sense of compassion. Other traits associated with this personality include:

●A crave for appreciation and acknowledgment even when nothing has been accomplished

●Appreciation of personal beauty and success

●A feeling of being better than others

●Exploit and manipulation of others

●Grandiosity and a high emphasis on self

●Fantasies of being critical, famous or influential

●Exaggeration of individual accomplishments and abilities

Notes:

_____

_____

_____

_____

_____

_____

_____

_____

_____

_____

_____

_____

_____

_____

_____

_____

_____

_____

_____

_____

_____

_____

_____

_____

_____

_____

_____

Narcissistic Fathers

Narcissistic Fathers

Chapter 4: Narcissistic Strategies of Manipulation

Narcissistic people are never logical. They never agree they are wrong and often throw tantrums when you try to call them out on their behavior. Most times, they try to manipulate you to get their way. These manipulation techniques are very subtle and can be challenging to spot. However, to properly ensure you don't fall for their antics, you need to learn to spot them.

In this section, we will be looking into some of the ways a narcissistic father tries to manipulate and how you can protect yourself.

Emotional Blackmail

Here the narcissistic seems to appeal to you for something. However, in reality, this is not an appeal but a demand, and if you refuse to do it, then you face a barrage of consequences. All of these are to ensure you agree to her request. If you fail to do what she wants, she will capitalize on many of the weapons in her arsenal to punish you. They will throw insults, give you the cold shoulder, withdraw affection and love, and even threaten you with physical violence. These are some forms of emotional abuse the narcissistic parent uses to control you.

For instance: Your narcissistic father may request that you leave all of your prior engagements and come for a program that is important to him. Because his proposed commitment is impromptu, and you already made plans way beforehand, you tell him you won't be able to make it along with your reasons.

Instead of trying to understand your perspectives and respecting your desires, he goes ahead to tell you how ungrateful you are for not being there when he needs you. If you still refuse to show up, he gives you the cold shoulder for weeks, or even months.

How to protect yourself: Set up boundaries and know the extent of these boundaries. You are allowed to reject any request or invitation if it does not fit your schedule. This becomes particularly important when dealing with a person who has toxic behavior. You have the right to reject requests. Refuse to fall for any cold shoulders or insults that may come your way.

If you live far away from your narcissistic father, an easier way is to keep your distance. Ensure you don't respond to text messages or emails they send to guilt-trip you. Say no and stand your ground no matter what happens.

He Uses Obligation and Fear to Guilt-Trip You

It is not strange for narcissistic parents to use fear and obligation to guilt-tip you into doing their bidding even if it does not align with your desires.

For instance: Your father is the owner of a renowned company, and he wants you to take the mantle. However, you have other plans for your life, and when you tell him you are happier doing something else, he lashes out and says, "What is going to happen to our family legacy? Is this how you want to repay me for all the sacrifices I made for you? You are a shame to the family, and you don't deserve our name!"

How to protect yourself: When a narcissist parent guilt trips, you understand that any shame or guilt that comes from it is not genuine. Remember that it is your right to have preferences and make choices, even if your narcissistic father does not support these choices. You don't need to explain to anyone about the options you make in your personal life, especially when they are only after their benefit.

Shaming

Narcissistic parents shame their kids to make them feel less about themselves. According to research, when a person feels imperfect and flawed, they are more likely to acquiesce to the demands of others. This is why it is a useful tool when in the hands of a narcissistic parent. They shame you with your personal information, whether publicly or privately, to make you more compliant with their desires.

For instance: Your narcissistic father starts to make snide comments about your choice of a partner during your family Christmas gathering. Even though your marriage is a successful one, and you are happy with your partner, they keep poking at your areas of imperfection all because you did not marry the woman they chose for you. They may continuously tell you how your marriage is going to fail and how you both won't make good parents.

How to protect yourself: Don't let your father continuous with this behavior. Try to keep the distance, and you will not show up as much for any events they will be part of. Instead of dwelling in shame, remember how far you have come, and how happy you are. Instead of being ashamed of yourself, acknowledge your areas of success, and take pride in them.

He Compares

We covered comparison earlier on. Narcissistic parents often compare their kids to others to make them feel less.

For instance: Your childhood friend comes over and tells you he just got a new well-paying job. Later on, your father asks you why you can't be more like your childhood friend, and also proceeds to ask what you are doing with your life.

How to protect yourself: You need to remember that all humans are different in areas they excel in. Do not let anyone draw you in with comparisons. Note that this is another strategy to make you feel less, and if you fall for it, you will only be making your narcissist parent win over you.

Instead of trying to make your father understand by listing out your achievements, don't bother. This is because he would still find a way to make them worthless anyway. You should channel your time and energy into hanging around people that support you and understand the value of what you have achieved. Don't compare yourself with other people to feel successful.

Notes:

_____

_____

_____

_____

_____

_____

_____

_____

_____

_____

_____

_____

_____

_____

_____

_____

_____

_____

_____

_____

_____

_____

_____

_____

_____

_____

Chapter 5: How a Narcissist can control you

Dealing with a narcissist means that every day could be a challenge. However, it helps if you know what to expect from them, so you won't end up disappointed.

A narcissist does not have any respect for you and your boundaries. They might even encourage talks against you, gossips about you, and fools you into believing that he or she is in love with you.

Promises are made to be broken, all the time. Narcissists make them, but will likely not honor them. When you confront them about it, they would vehemently deny it. They might even feel indignant by saying how dare you for thinking that they did something wrong by forgetting their promise. They might even blame you and your "high standards" for the fact that they failed to realize their promise.

A narcissist will only do something if they know they can get something out of it. They won't mow the lawn, wash the dishes, or run errands for you if they know that these things will not get appreciated or rewarded for it. They always want to be credited for everything that they do. If it goes unnoticed, prepare to listen to their ranting about it.

Humility is definitely out of reach, and their priority will always be themselves. They are not even ashamed of being selfish and feeling entitled.

They do not recognize boundaries. Narcissists are used to crossing personal boundaries if it means getting to their goal. It could be to hurt you or another person, and they won't apologize for it.

Narcissists are not capable of loving and caring. They do have feelings, but these are all based on certain conditions. Usually, they will show the motions of loving you if they know that you can boost their ego by supporting their grandiose view of themselves. If you disagree with them, then don't expect them to show their fake love and warmth.

The narcissist lives to trigger emotional reactions in people because, in their minds, that gives them some sense of power. If a narcissist causes you to lose control over your emotions, it gives him a lot of satisfaction. When a narcissist attacks you verbally, ignoring him can drive him crazy.

You have to understand that narcissists crave attention, so ignoring them hurts them more than anything else. They want to be acknowledged and validated; that is why they start with the conflict in the first place. When a narcissist targets you and destroys your life, your natural instinct will be to get back at him/her by reacting angrily and emotionally, but if you do that, you are only playing into his/her hand.

It may not seem so at first. Still, over time, you will realize that ignoring the narcissist is much more satisfying than engaging with him/her because then, even to third-party observers, the narcissist will just seem like a petty person who likes to pick fights with people. You will look like a mature adult who can rise above it all.

The narcissist wants to control you and to assert dominance over you, but you have to remember that people can't take power from you. You have to give it to them. A narcissist can only dominate you if you relinquish control to him/her. As we have mentioned, you are guaranteed to lose if you play the narcissist's game, and that is when he/she is capable of dominating you. By ignoring the narcissist, you blatantly refuse to perform his/her game, and then he/she has no means with which to get close enough to have any form of control over your life.

Notes:

_____
_____
_____
_____
_____
_____
_____
_____
_____
_____
_____
_____
_____
_____
_____
_____
_____
_____
_____
_____
_____
_____
_____
_____
_____
_____
_____

Narcissistic Fathers

Chapter 6: Manipulation Technique

Gaslighting is one of the most effective standard tool narcissists use. It includes narcissistic parents too. This is a kind of emotional abuse where the father continuously makes up stories to distort the reality of the victim, which is the child in this case.

Soon, the victim begins to be unsure of his or her instincts and would completely believe the reality of the abuser, even if the child has proof of these answers.

Calling out the toxic parent for their behavior becomes impossible with gaslighting as the victim will be conditioned to believe they are the toxic ones if they do. Victims of gaslighting have a higher probability of dealing with other kinds of abuse, as well.

For instance: Your narcissistic father asks you to do something for him that would result in you going out of your way. You tell him why this would be impossible as you already have a lot on your plate. Rather than understanding and respecting your wishes, he continues to push and pester you to do his bidding. When you still fail to comply, he goes ahead to punish you with snide comments and insults, even in the presence of others.

The next day when you believe the situation must have calmed down, you try to call him out on her behavior the day before. Instead of admitting and apologizing his wrong, he responds with, "You are over-reacting, I never insulted you. Perhaps you are creating events in your mind."

If, in any case, you try to encounter him about something he has done, he insults you telling you that you have a vivid imagination. This is common across all sorts of narcissists to invalidate your experience over your abuse. He also abuses you that she can't understand what you are talking about. He pretends to forget about very memorable events denying like it never happened, and when you remind him, he does not admit of any possibility that he might have forgotten. This tactic is referred to as "gaslighting," and entails a very aggressive and exceptionally infuriating behavior that is common across all sorts of narcissists. He undermines your perceptions of reality, which kills your confidence in your reasoning power, your memory, and intuition, which makes you a complete victim to him.

Moreover, narcissistic fathers are always gaslight. You will hear them telling you that you are unstable to listen to certain things. They refer to you as over-reactive, completely unreasonable, hysterical, always imagining, or oversensitive.

Once he has constructed these false fantasies of your emotional pathologies, he will share them with others, showing them how helpless and a victim he is with you around him. He always claims to be innocent and states that he ultimately doesn't understand why you are so angry with him. You end up being the one who hurt him and thinks that you need psychotherapy. He claims how much he loves and cares about you and would do anything to see you happy, but he doesn't understand how. According to him, all you do is pushing him when all he wanted was to help you. He complains that he has sacrificed his responsibilities for your empathy and concludes that something is wrong about you. He uses this as a weapon to undermine your credibility with his listeners by clearly elaborating how perfect he plays his role as a father.

How to Protect Yourself: Individuals who suffer from gaslighting tend to doubt everything and hardly do anything by themselves. This goes on until adulthood. As opposed to allowing yourself to be conditioned, don't give in. Remember that everything your narcissistic parent wants you to believe is not the truth. Find your reality and hold on to it.

To ensure you don't forget, keeping a journal at this point would be a great idea. Anytime your parent abuses you, write it down so you can remember the original version even when they try to gaslight you later on. Do not live by the reality your narcissistic parent tries to plant. If you do, you would be less likely to prevent yourself from being exploited.

No one deserves to be exposed to emotional abuse or manipulation of any form. Stand your ground and resist it as much as you can.

Note 1: Part 1 of this book is taken from *"Narcissistic Mothers: A practical guide for Daughter and Son to recognize a Narcissistic Parent Abuse and how to heal and recover from CPTSD"*, adapting the text on the subject of this book.

Notes:

_____

_____

_____

_____

_____

_____

_____

_____

_____

_____

_____

_____

_____

_____

_____

_____

_____

_____

_____

_____

_____

_____

_____

_____

_____

_____

_____

Narcissistic Fathers

PART TWO: TRAITS OF NARCISSISTIC FATHERS

Chapter 1: The Narcissistic Father

Narcissistic fathers affect the lives of their children; as a child and as an adult. Their relationships, work, and entire lives are negatively affected. The critical part is that adult children with narcissistic fathers may not easily decipher what is wrong even till death.

In most cases, the narcissistic dad suffers from NPD (Narcissistic Personality Disorder), which might not be detected early. A father with NPD exposes his child(ren) to a world of abuse, which can be mild and extreme. A Narcissistic father sees his child as a means to boost his ego; he sees him/her as an extension and not a person.

The truth is that we are all a tad narcissistic. Many of us balance out the narcissism with humility. Why do our fathers fail at humility for balance? According to some studies, narcissism is a taught behavior in childhood. Probably the boy child was coddled just a little too much, or maybe his parents took care of things for him rather than allow him to stand on his own two feet. Perhaps there was praise for doing something wrong or the idea that "boys will be boys" was drilled daily in his mind. And rather than correct and teach him some humility, it kept going well into adulthood.

Now you have someone who does not know how to function in any other capacity, your father!

Even as the child grows, the dad, being a narcissist, feels the need to gain control over his child. This leads to competition and extends to jealousy. Since the narcissistic dad is interested in gaining control, he might view his child growing independence as a threat. Therefore, the threatened narcissistic dad decides to bully and abuse the helpless child. What seemed like love and admiration from a narcissistic father suddenly turns to anger and resentment. In some cases, a narcissistic rage can become violent or physical, leading to physical injuries in the case of boys or rape in the case of girls.

To stay out of trouble, most children decide to adhere to the rules of their narcissistic dad. They avoid the narcissistic rage by trying to adjust their lives to suit the needs of their father. Most times, the abused child is made to believe that the cause of the problem lies in him/her. He thinks, "well, maybe I am a bad person, after all."

The child lives through this emotional trauma for most of his life. He knows something is wrong, but since he can figure out what it is, he concludes that maybe that is how parents are.

However, the picture above is just one manifestation of narcissistic dads. Some fathers can be nice, friendly, kind, and loving to you. But, a narcissist love comes with conditions. Narcissist fathers are always self-centered, and their needs come first. If they show you love, on the one hand, they will make you feel guilty or beholden on the other hand. The child grows up feeling that all forms of love are conditional.

The major problem with the children of a narcissistic father is the confusion that stems from not understanding what the problem is, yet they know something is not right. Even when some children are exposed to the traits and find that it is similar to their father, they still feel that they are the cause of the problem. This is the extent of child abuse and brainwashing done to them while they were young.

How did this develop over the years?

1. Children whose dads are narcissistic have been taught, over the years, that all they do is a reflection of their father. So, if the narcissistic father had shown, conditional love, he/she is compelled to fit into his lifestyle. Also, if the narcissistic father had shown anger and contempt, he/she is afraid to be like him.

2. Both mentality further increases the problem and makes the child extremely anxious. The child is scared of what he wants. On one side of the narcissistic father, he is anxious to measure up. On the other side, he is eager to get away from any path that reveals his father's character.

3. This identity crisis becomes confusing to the child, and he/she concludes that everything is his/her fault. The shame of the abused child increases further since he/she has never had unconditional love.

Manipulations used by Narcissistic Fathers

Parentification

This is a form of role reversal; the child is forced to care for his father while the father, through emotional blackmail, plays the role of a child. The most child feels compelled to help their parent while they give up the love and care that they need as a child.

Infantilization

Where parentification makes a child feels obligated to act like the adult, infantilization keeps the child caged even when he/she is an adult. Narcissistic fathers usually do this with their daughters. Infantilization is very degrading and can slow down the progress of the adult whose father is a chronic narcissist.

Triangulation

This is a strategy used by narcissistic fathers in passing information and separating siblings. The narcissistic father maintains his grandiosity by passing information indirectly. Narcissistic dads, while he attempts to mask his rage, tell the golden child what he thinks about the scapegoat. Of course, this will create strife among the siblings, but the narcissistic father remains the unaffected one.

Hoovering

Have you ever wondered why it is so difficult to maintain strict boundaries with your narcissistic dad? Yes, the "Hoover Maneuver" manipulation was used to get you back. Once the narcissistic father realizes that you have successfully distant yourself from him, he pulls out this trick. In most cases, it is through victimization, emotional blackmail, or any subtle lie that keeps you at his beck and call.

Gaslighting

Children often grow up with the belief that parents do not lie. In reality, for the most part, parents distort reality to their children. Many fathers do not know how they gaslight their kids. Narcissistic father uses this weapon frequently, most especially when their children's independence threatens them. Terms like, "that's not how it is done," "I know you better than you know yourself," "I am your father, I know what is right for you," are examples of how narcissistic dads gaslight their kids.

Projecting

Narcissistic fathers win the blame game confidently by projecting. If the plate slips from his hand, you probably did not wash it well. Most kids realize this, but they are forced to believe that they need to do better to make things right. A narcissistic father cannot allow people to see their flaws and weaknesses. Therefore, their kids become the perfect place to dump the blame.

Terms you should know about Narcissistic Fathers

Narcissistic Attachment

When narcissists have kids, they view them as a way to improve their ego, self-esteem, and lifestyle. The narcissistic attachment has been part of a narcissist before they give birth. They attach their self-worth to others through avoidant attachments style or anxious attachment style.

Narcissistic Injury

Narcissistic dads are scared of open criticisms. They are more vulnerable when the criticism is from their child. This public criticism opens up the hidden narcissistic wound. The narcissist is always protecting and projecting his vain ego. To hit on his ego and dominance is to cause a narcissistic injury, which leads to rage.

Narcissistic Supply

A narcissist craves for attention. As a father, he wants to control everything and everyone; and he wants to be admired for it. Narcissistic supply, a term introduced in 1938, is the source where the narcissist gets unlimited attention. The narcissistic dad gets his supply by instilling fear in the child or gaining control of the child's decisions.

Narcissistic rage

The narcissist rage is the result of his injury or when his narcissistic supply has been cut of. The best way to know a narcissistic father is when you decide to go your way or openly challenge his decision. Narcissistic rage can be very aggressive and violent

How Your Father Became a Narcissist

Your father did not become a narcissist after giving birth to you. This would only mean that all parents are a narcissist. Narcissistic behaviors are formed from different factors that are yet to be proven by researchers. Naturally, many psychoanalysts believe that NPD (Narcissistic Personality Disorder) is formed majorly by environmental factors, i.e., the narcissist is not born but made. However, there have been little signs of genetics and neurobiological factors.

Environmental Factors

Many narcissistic dads grow up in an environment that fuels their behavior. One major thing you must note is that your narcissistic dad probably grew up with a narcissistic parent.

Parents who are fond of placing their child above every other child create a false sense of self in them, which would eventually lead to grandiose narcissism. The society which places a high value on performance can also create a narcissistic personality. Also, social media contribute a lot to this personality disorder.

Genetic Factors

Genetic factors contribute a little part in developing a narcissistic personality. Ultimately, the major part where genes matter in narcissism is when narcissistic people date and marry each other or people with different unstable characters. The truth is, it is almost difficult for any child, even with the healthiest traits, to grow without issues when dysfunction gets married to another dysfunction.

Neurobiological factors

Recent research concluded that Narcissistic people have abnormal cerebral cortex slimness in the area essential for empathy development as compared to individuals who do not have a personality disorder. The study also maintained that the level of compassion missed in narcissistic people matches the degree of slimness in the unusual region of the cerebral cortex.

Types of Narcissistic Fathers

There are two distinct types of narcissistic fathers. Engulfing fathers who may be overt narcissists as well as ignoring fathers who may be subtle narcissists. Each of these Narcissistic behavior shown by fathers is extremely harmful to their children. It is crucial to understand this distinct personality so that you can quickly heal yourself and become the father of that lonely kid within you:

The Overtly Engulfing Father

These are Narcissistic Fathers who do not see any distinction between their kids and themselves. The overt engulfing dad finds it hard to view their child as another person. This is not a problem for newborns because small children still never really see themselves as different from their dad. The overt narcissistic father is easily detected when they appear to be noisy, rude, and disrespectful to other people's desires and always hungry for praise.

Methods such as Parentification, Infantilization, and Triangulation are manipulations used by an overtly engulfing father in attaching himself to his child. As a grows, this type of narcissistic dad will ignore all borders, seeing no issue asking excessively intrusive questions, reading their child's private messages, and individual stories. Through their relationships with everyone, they show more extroverted attitudes.

An overt engulfing father can be very flamboyant. He claims his grandiose openly and proclaims that "nobody is greater than me." Their flamboyance makes them easy to notice.

Some overtly engulfing fathers are substance abusers making them the hardest types of narcissists. This is because the combination of substance abuse and narcissism is very destructive. Even when the drunken engulfing father is sober, the child is still emotionally attached through parentification.

The Covertly Ignoring Father

These are narcissistic fathers who don't really mind much for their kids. But, they are not loud about it. A Covert Ignoring father recognizes the barrier between himself and his child and does not care at all. These fathers can be spotted in the crowd, exchanging fantastic stories with smooth voices that create a feeling of value and achievement to feel adored. Behind the doors, with their kids, they don't bother much.

These are narcissists who express the same self-centered qualities with an engulfing father but without any externally defining features. This trait can be incredibly frustrating and confusing as the kid grows up feeling lonely, unloved, making it, or the child build any healthy relationship in the future. A Covertly Ignoring dad often does everything well except for his child. He is not even aware of his child's health, neatness, hygiene, or school assignments.

These fathers, regardless of their interest, demand top achievements from their kids. They command respect in public and want their children to do the same, a way to boost their social presence. The slogan for their family is that "We are Special." Most children from these backgrounds strive endlessly to meet the requirements of their highly-placed dad.

Other covertly ignoring fathers are secretly mean to their children. Since they have an ego to protect in public, they decide to hide their abusive tendencies from the public. Everyone sees them are lovely people, but you know who they are, and your story will be an attempt to bring them down negatively.

Notes:

_____
_____
_____
_____
_____
_____
_____
_____
_____
_____
_____
_____
_____
_____
_____
_____
_____
_____
_____
_____
_____
_____
_____
_____
_____
_____
_____

Chapter 2: Signs That You Were Raised by a Narcissistic Father

Figuring out how to comprehend and make harmony with your adolescence is the best way to heal yourself quickly. When you have lived with a narcissistic dad for long, it will seriously influence your mental improvement, changing your thinking, emotional, moral frame of mind. But, how can we even recognize that we grew up with a Narcissistic Father?

It is somewhat troublesome because everyone perceives your father as an overwhelming social magnet who pulls in individuals from varying backgrounds. But, in secret, all affectation falls away. A narcissistic dad could be affected by Narcissism or NPD (Narcissistic Personality Disorder). Commonly, narcissistic dads are possessively near to their kids and eventually become troubled by their kids' developing autonomy.

Growing up under the watch of a narcissist makes us think, for most of our lives, that we are simply not "sufficient" regardless of all our effort to satisfy others. Being the child, you are the one who realizes what it feels like to persevere through their virus character for quite a long time over a minor infraction or endure the worst part of consistent, age-long requests for flawlessness and quality. You recognize what it feels like to be parented by a narcissist, dad.

NPD (Narcissistic Personality Disorder) is one of 10 character issues portrayed in the Diagnostic and Statistical Manual of Mental Disorders, a legitimate mental guide. Individuals with narcissistic character issues might be commonly troubled and disillusioned when they're not given the unique favors or profound respect they think they merit. They are consistently infatuated with their swelled mental self-portrait, definitely because it enables them to disguise the extent of their insecurity.

Even though scientists revealed that less than one percent of the US population has extreme Narcissistic Personality Disorder, yet somewhere in the range of two to 16 percent of individuals who look for treatment have such character flaws. Different specialists have discovered that narcissistic people have higher paces of self-ending treatment. NPD is a group B character disorder, which is portrayed by sensational, excessively passionate, or capricious reasoning or conduct.

Yet, the offspring of narcissists are seldom in a situation to request that their folks look for help. Numerous grown-up offspring of narcissistic guardians experience difficulty relinquishing their needs for their folks. Truth be told, they may not understand that their folks were narcissists until they look for proficient assistance for their battles. It bodes well; all things considered, we are naturally modified to bond with our folks, and the connections we structure as youngsters are what wire our minds to assist us with framing secure connections later on. However, below, I will reveal how you can decipher if you grew up with a narcissistic father.

Lack of Self-Esteem

Narcissistic dads frequently and genuinely harm their kids. Such a father will stomp on all over their family to address their wants without really thinking about what any other individual needs. Furthermore, they dismiss limits, control their kids by retaining friendship, and disregard to address the issues of their kids since they are intrigued distinctly with regards to addressing their very own needs.

Along these lines, some grown-up offspring of narcissists will try to attain perfection to ensure nobody would be able to criticize them. Huge numbers of the grown-up offspring of narcissists studied revealed re-thinking themselves, their encounters, and their decisions. They rapidly discover that all that they do is an impression of the narcissistic dad. They adjust their conduct to satisfy their father, and they disregard their own needs. They let individuals abuse them since they're not in contact with what they need, and they don't know to let it out.

To conquer this, find out as much about Narcissism as you can, to have the option to distinguish the lies you grew up with, and start neutralizing them. You will rapidly discover that not every person who appears to be keen on you is interested in you for honorable reasons. Henceforth, you would be cautious about the amount of yourself you uncover to individuals. People got narcissistic, in any event to a limited extent, by disguising their dads' expanded thoughts of them — and narcissistic fathers are infamous for doing precisely that.

Fear of Turning into a Narcissist

Some kids see that the best way to maintain a strategic distance from derision and misuse is to resemble their narcissistic father. Throughout the years, this endurance strategy transforms into how they really observe the world.

Grown-up offspring of narcissists need to undermine or become overachieving sticklers trying to keep away from the constant criticism they were exposed to while they with their father. An absence of confidence drives children of narcissistic dads. Due to trying hard to earn validation from their dad, the kid may never get the chance to understand himself. Inevitably, they become profoundly hesitant to talk without hesitating or confront others.

To overcome this, look for the assistance of a therapist or friend to assist you with breaking out of injurious personal conduct standards, most importantly, when you are in a relationship or have children. You need individuals to remind you what adulthood is about at times, and you need a keen ear to converse with about what you are experiencing. You will have a full scope of feelings and contemplations about this circumstance. Discover and interface with other Adult Children of Narcissistic Parents. Discover an advisor who spends significant time in treating Adult Children of Narcissistic fathers.

You are Competitive

Narcissists experience difficulty with individual limits and view others as augmentations of themselves. In families with a few youngsters, one might be picked to mirror the Narcissist's best characteristics. Raised by an arrogant, focused, presumptuous dad, they have an inclination that they can never have the goods or are sufficient to collect their dad's endorsement. They get the most consideration, applause, and backing, but at the same time are under the most strain to perform. Narcissistic guardians have exclusive requirements of their kids — and a lot of them.

However, Narcissist plays a game on their children. While one child has been praised for no reason, another child may be a target for the parent's blame and shame and scapegoated as a burden that can never do anything right compared to the chosen child. These further enhance the extent of competition in the family.

When Narcissist fathers place the loved kid over the rebellious child, the competition gives room to separation among the sibling. Nevertheless, you must remember that no matter who you are to a Narcissistic father, the whole show (positive or negative) is for his inflated ego. So, you have to make peace with your sibling with your new information on who your father really is. Make your sibling understand that the praises from a narcissist father are never out of love but selfishness.

Naturally, there would have been so much love lost between you and your brother/sister. In most cases, the spouse of a narcissist father does not help the situation as she has been brutally abused. Extreme Narcissistic fathers enjoy watching as the family drama unfolds, which makes it challenging to bridge the gap between you and your siblings. But, if the children can find a way to fish out the primary source of their family woes, being the Narcissistic father, they will bond to each other for life.

You are Obligated to Help People at all Cost

There are different types of Narcissism. While some are rash, others are soft, subtly playing the victim. Naturally, when a narcissist discovers that there are fewer cards to draw you with, they resort to their last manipulative weapon -- Emotional blackmail. The narcissistic father decides to threaten you with harming themselves, except you do what they ask for. This request is not always evident. Sometimes, it comes out of a soft, pleading voice in distress.

If you have lived with this type of father all your life, you might be stuck on helping other people at the expense of your happiness. This is because when you stay around unfulfilled people for a long time, you will find it difficult to move ahead because there is always someone to help. I have heard people narrate how they don't want to invoke their father's wrath with one decision or the other. In the end, this will become a real burden for the child throughout his life.

It all starts with the narcissistic sense of drama, which develops because the Narcissistic dad can face reality. Such a man because emotional and angry randomly because he is stuck on his past failures and regrets. You don't have to be compelled to please such a person because you would be forced to continue satisfying his needs. As a result, you would find yourself apologizing for everything, anything, and nothing. This will affect all your relationships because you would become addicted to living with dramatic and self-centered people. Living with calm people, who love you unconditionally will become boring.

How can you deal with this? You need to go back to the days when you were young. This is not for the purpose of reminiscing but reconstructing. You need to discover the child in you and start re-parenting him/her. You can begin this by imagining your childhood days. Always remind yourself that the little boy or girl in you lacked a good father, which you will now play such a role.

You Define Your Worth on Performance

One significant effect of being the child of a narcissistic father is that you become who they are. This is why you must seek help quickly (probably from a therapist). If you have been compelled to define your self-worth by performance, after a while, you would demand the same from others. This explains why some people are addicted to work, which will also affect their relationships as they strive unnecessarily to meet the standards of the Narcissist dad.

To free yourself from the circle of never-ending work and stop defining yourself based on what you can achieve, empathize with your narcissistic father. Understand that your Narcissistic dad lacks empathy and finds it hard to notice other people's feelings. Also, remember that even when you achieve to please him, he is not concerned about what you went through. Any achievement to earn his validation can only inflate his ego. So, you should stop working endlessly to please such a cold character.

The more a child suffers from a narcissistic father, the more the damage done to his personality. For instance, a child that gets criticized continuously or praised by his father will eventually work twice hard to earn more praise or avoid the slightest criticism. The child's self-esteem is severely damaged, and he/she needs to hide it. It is not so easy to rebuild the damaged esteem but understand that it is your responsibility to start rebuilding even though you had no idea how you turned out that way.

You are Never Decisive

One thing you can't take from a Narcissistic dad is his grandiose. He needs to feel better than everyone around, and he needs to have his say and way. Narcissistic dads overestimate their strengths. However, the painful reality is that they can never achieve such grandiose, and hence, they attempt to accomplish this in their household.

When you see your dad as an elite, which he acts like, it becomes difficult for you to know exactly what you want. You might find out this flawed character, but you just assume that every dad behaves in this manner. This is revealed in the way many children regret their choice of career. Other people later discover that they picked a career because it reflected the character of their dad.

The best way to overcome your problem of indecisiveness is by maintaining a reasonable distance with your narcissistic dad. Reduce the time you spend with them and stop feeling bad about it. You might discover that your father is not even narcissistic but, once you keep feeling trapped around him, it is best to avoid him. The problem most children face is believing that their narcissistic father would change in the future. It is an illusion you need to abandon if you want to start making decisions comfortably on your own.

Notes:

_____

_____

_____

_____

_____

_____

_____

_____

_____

_____

_____

_____

_____

_____

_____

_____

_____

_____

_____

_____

_____

_____

_____

_____

_____

_____

Chapter 3: How Kids Experience Narcissistic Fathers

Narcissistic dads create an atmosphere of pressure among all relatives; Sometimes it is secretly done but damaging for the children. They will use manipulation techniques to divide siblings, they adjust reality, they make misleading comments, and you begin to see the theme, much the same as in a sentimental relationship, of how they make that disarray.

NPD (Narcissistic Personality Disorder) is characterized as the worst form of self-importance with a requirement for esteem, an absence of compassion, and a feeling of privilege. Several psychologists have a wide range of speculations about whether narcissism is a severe personality issue, a hereditary inclination, or a blend of the two. Be that as it may, what is evident is how narcissist's acts, which can be so disastrous for those near them.

Divisions in the Family (Golden and Scapegoat Child)

In many narcissistic families, siblings naturally assume roles imposed on them by their father. For example, narcissistic dads are excessively critical, even though they need their kids to sustain their own sense of self. How this shows occurs in two unmistakable manners.

The narcissistic father treats siblings differently in an unexpected way - frequently, one is the favored kid, and one is the substitute. You'll see narcissistic fathers go to each school occasion, each game, each role the favored kid partakes in, and never appear at anything for the scapegoat.

It's challenging to cultivate any valid sibling association in that condition since they're being utilized as pawns by their dad. When the unfavored youngster attempts to discuss what their life resembles with the narcissistic parent, the most loved kid won't be there to listen.

This causes pressure and "cliques" inside families, because the favored kid may just consider the scapegoat to be as desirous of their consideration.

Through unexpected adoration, gaslighting, quiet treatment, and control, a few dads cause siblings a lot of mischiefs. The narcissistic father would castigate one kin to the next one. It doesn't appear to be more right than wrong to the prodigy, yet he/she is committed to tuning in to all the messy talks.

It deteriorates further when the enabling wife (your mother) adds to the maltreatment by tuning in to her kids' issues, at that point, enlightening your dad regarding them, somewhat acting like a snitch.

The spouse is entangled with her husband and doesn't appear to comprehend where his sentiments end and hers start. In that capacity, she frequently goes about as his witness and, in some cases, as her ax-man. The wife is calm and great at tuning in and will give you the impression she's your ally, at that point, return and disclose to her husband all that you imparted to her in certainty.

Narcissists treat individuals like pawns on a chessboard. It does not change with their spouses and children. The ideal situation is that the kin grows up having some attention to the circumstance. Afterward, they can present appropriate reparations with one another and set up sound limits together. In any case, this doesn't generally occur.

Unfortunately, it is the ill-favored kid who needs to help instruct that favored youngster regarding what occurred, and that can be a complicated issue to mend since the latter believes that the former is only jealous of him/her.

If there isn't any definite scholarly or athletic purpose behind one youngster to be the top pick, a narcissistic man will, in some cases, pick his scapegoat if he/she brings memories of his failings. Some studies revealed that 'Shame' is a piece of what makes a narcissist, and if they see their very own portion frailties, perceived shortcomings, or defects in their kid, they may sincerely dismiss them for it.

Narcissists attempt to imagine that they are great. They would prefer not to perceive any of their defects and address the reality they are merely ordinary because, in their mind, they are unrivaled.

By reflecting back on their own humankind, the narcissist's feeling of self is compromised. Thus, they unleash their rage.

Are Narcissists Capable of Loving Their Kids?

What narcissistic dads experience or profess is far from love. There will be snapshots of perceived love, like celebrations with excellent presents, or costly summer occasions. In any case, eventually, the cover will unavoidably fall, and the benevolence will wane.

Narcissistic dads need kids since they accept they will get more out of the relationship than they do. In any case, child upbringing is the most magnanimous activity you will ever have, and the unreasonable desires can prompt narcissistic anger when a kid grows up and turns into their own individual.

In the long haul, being raised by a narcissistic dad influences how kids structure their very own connections and build up their connection styles. Equally, it can be directed at disentangling that awful start. Toxic dads can push our buttons superior to anybody since they made it themselves — for example, moments when the father decides to have some fun with the scapegoat youngster.

Some of the time, they will simply grasp the job that they're an agitator or a mess up because that is the message that narcissistic dad has given them. In treatment, the offspring of narcissistic dads need to make a stride back and ask themselves whether they need to remain that pawn on the chessboard or not.

Human behavior is created within a setting, gathering odds and ends of the connections in our society to join them, unknowingly, to our demeanor—that wired-in natural blueprint that, in part, reveals who we become. This is how any character is born.

What develops and reshapes our personality when we are raised in the toxic world of a narcissistic dad? Below are some effects of living with a narcissistic father:

Self-Blame that is damaging

Narcissistic dads could possibly be very harsh. However, they're very likely oblivious of their children's emotions. They are excessively engrossed with their very own worries to hear our torment. Since genuinely delicate kids who long for affection can't just exit the entryway and locate another family, they regularly sustain trust by yielding their confidence. They place the blame on themselves. The sensitive child thinks if he were calmer, more settled, or more joyful, his father wouldn't shout on him/her; overlook or reprimand him constantly. The child believes that he/she is the one that needs to change for things to change.

Resounding Others without Personal Opinion

In case you're exceptionally touchy or empathic, mostly, you're bound to react to narcissistic upbringing with a position called echoism, named after the fairy Echo (Echo was a mountain fairy that lived on Mount Kithaironan in Greek mythology). Echo was reviled to rehash back the last scarcely any words she heard. Similarly, as Narcissus was crazy for his appearance, Echo began to look all starry eyed at Narcissus. Narcissistic dads who detonate abruptly or breakdown in tears whenever a kid sets out to express a need, compel their kids to occupy as meager space as could reasonably be expected, as though having any desires whatsoever is a demonstration of narrow-mindedness. The child does not have his opinion and eventually ends up in a similar relationship.

Forming Unstable Relationships

The disregard, misuse, or emotional absence of a narcissistic parent can make us question how safe we are in others' grasp. Generally, the uncertain relationship can take two structures:

Avoidant connection, in which we deal with our feelings of trepidation by closing individuals out;

Edge connection, where we pursue love, seeking after—here and there irately—the association we long for with our friends and family;

Regardless of whether you become on edge or avoidant relies upon an intricate mix of personality and consistency in care and consideration, however progressing disregard will, in general, make evasion, and unusual consideration, for the most part, yields tension.

Becoming Extremely Needy and Helpless

Narcissistic dads can make their kids scared of their needs, which cover them by turning out to be habitual guardians or essentially falling quiet. They may murmur along for some time, appearing to require nothing from their accomplices or companions. At that point, an emergency hits, and all of a sudden—in manners they find profoundly agitating—they call their companions unendingly or look for consistent consolation. The fastest method to wipe out a need is to get it met promptly; incomprehensibly, the individuals generally scared of their needs can appear the most "penniless."

Wild freedom

Active, courageous youngsters may react to narcissistic child-rearing by deserting enthusiastic closeness, by and large, accepting that nobody can be trusted or depended on. This is difficult to continue, usually, and can without much of a stretch cause discontinuous need alarm. Then again, kids with increasingly delicate demeanors may turn out to be enthusiastically benevolent guardians, as though the main way they can appreciate nurturance is vicarious, by giving others the glow and minding they never delighted in.

Having an Unfair Responsibility

Inconsistently delicate youngsters can build up a laser-like spotlight on their fathers and later, their accomplices' needs. They sort out their lives around the joy of others, persuaded they need to support their folks' regard, or anticipate their next blast by intently disapproving of their every craving or impulse. The alarmed youngster turned minimal grown-up frequently grows up to stress perpetually over their self-centeredness. They may even develop to detest their own needs, seeing them as a weight to other people.

Developing Extraordinary Narcissism

The more forceful a kid is, the more he reacts to narcissistic parental abuse by playing around the idea that "if you can't beat them, go along with them." He says to himself, "I'll simply ensure I'm the most intense, prettiest, sharpest individual in the room. That way, nobody can make me feel immaterial once more." If you're brought into the world with a problematic, ranting personality and exposed to the sort of careless or harsh upbringing narcissists regularly give, you're bound to wind up narcissistic yourself.

Post-Traumatic Stress Disorder (PTSD).

The more damaging a narcissistic dad becomes, the more he is to damage their kids. That can prompt a dreadful way to deal with life and eventually lead to Post-Traumatic Stress Disorder.

Parental abuse tosses people into a condition of consistent readiness, carefully arranged to evade the following peril.

This regularly prompts interminable tension, an abrupt flashback of abuse, loss of emotions, and even a feeling of uncertainty for the future, wherein individuals become so fixed on just enduring that they lose the capacity to envision life past the present.

One patient that went through parental abuse from a narcissistic father said that he wouldn't see his 30th birthday celebration. When living your life in constant fear of what will happen next, there's no space for a five-year plan. The future gets shapeless, even murky, and when that occurs, mapping out the next stages in life is similar to running into a wall.

Notes:

_____
_____
_____
_____
_____
_____
_____
_____
_____
_____
_____
_____
_____
_____
_____
_____
_____
_____
_____
_____
_____
_____
_____
_____
_____
_____
_____

Chapter 4: Narcissistic Father with their Daughter

Individuals who have been raised by a narcissistic parent can affirm how destructive both mentally and physically. Narcissistic guardians show no sympathy.

They want to micromanage the lives of their kids. They may neglect them as well as expose them to both physical and emotional maltreatment.

Daughters living with narcissistic dads spend their childhood dealing with an un-empathic, unfeeling, and abusive parent; however, alongside these, they may likewise experience special triggers and obstructions when recuperating.

Below are three regular difficulties that these little daughters live with and tips on the best way to move past them in the recuperating journey. Male children of narcissistic dads may likewise experience these.

The gaudy mental self-portrait and notoriety of their fathers typically don't coordinate with the coldness and nonchalance displayed when away from the public, habituating their youngsters to view interpersonal danger as the standard.

Narcissists are experts at managing impressions, and the same is true for the charismatic, narcissistic fathers. As the girl of a narcissistic dad, you may have seen that your dad places more value on his notoriety in the society over the comfort or happiness of you and your relatives.

Your dad was doubtlessly known as liberal, amicable, and uncommonly enchanting to each one of the individuals who knew him in the society, yet away from view, he was verbally and physically harsh to his life partner and kids.

This isn't exceptional in families with a narcissistic parent; their 'bogus self' is never in harmony with their genuine self-inside the domain of the family.

Subsequently, daughters of narcissistic fathers are told to keep their mouths shut should they ever have endeavored to take a stand in opposition and speak out about the challenges they go through. This, along with the prevailing gender orientation that women should be hushed-up, coy, and affable, daughters of narcissistic dads may have been molded to adjust to harm as opposed to shielding themselves from it.

That is the reason dangerous circumstances and individuals with a Jekyll and Hyde character – individuals who are seldom steady in their character or trustworthiness – appear like a familiar (perilous) haven to daughters of narcissistic fathers, when they grow.

How to do with this issue

Approve and recognize the encounters you had with your narcissistic father and don't permit the assessments of others to shadow the truth of the maltreatment you encountered.

It is a thing for survivors of any type of maltreatment to question themselves and become unsure of the awful infringement they encountered.

This is usually the case when their abuser is an adored person in society or displays himself as a caring and loving individual.

It is also likely that they have been immensely Gaslighted by their abusers, relatives, or companions of the family. Survivors of narcissistic maltreatment do 'gaslight' themselves into accepting their encounters were not legitimate, because of the notoriety of the abusers.

Do not allow the abuse to continue to affect your emotional well-being and mental health negatively; think about limiting contact with your abusive parent to just occasions and important events.

This empowers you to take your power back, as you can control the intervals with which you communicate with the parent and leave before dangerous situations reach boiling points.

A few survivors find that their own circumstance demands to avoid the abusive parent totally; if that is the situation, realize that you don't need to feel regretful or embarrassed.

Shielding yourself from dangerous individuals is both your right and duty, regardless of whether they share your genes.

Learn helpful approaches to self-approve. Keep a diary or talk with an advisor about the maltreatment you suffered to reconnect with it.

Discuss with relatives or companions who are understanding or who were likewise survivors of the maltreatment. Respect what you survived and understand that you didn't merit it in any way or structure.

Discover ways through which you can give yourself the emotional and mental care you required but couldn't get when you were young.

'Re-parent' yourself with sweet words, activities, and demonstrations of radical self-care that can help battle the damaging childhood you had.

Create a link to your internal identity through visualization, self-soothing, and meditation.

Recognize and consider constraining your relationship with any individual in your present personal sphere who has a 'bogus self' that doesn't line up with who they really are.

As a result of having a narcissistic father, we will generally gravitate towards individuals who feed us void words and bogus guarantees, or who are unavailable, emotionally.

One tends to become 'tone-deaf' to verbal and psychological mistreatment. Therefore, it is essential to perceive any toxic mode of communication we may likewise be enduring from our other relatives, companions, colleagues, and dates and then create boundaries that regard how we should be treated.

Lastly, guarantee that you're your true self – respect yourself and everything that makes up your personality.

Realize that you don't have to conceal your actual self from others and that you don't need to emulate your abusive dad's example in constantly seeking and to rely upon public validation.

Self-validation and being your real self is vital to your recuperating process. We will be unable to change the narcissistic parent. Yet, we can find a way to guarantee that we are living good lives and not displaying the parent's damaging methods for identifying with society.

The love halted once little girls arrived at adolescence, or it might have trespassed the limits. It is normal for parents and their young ones to have disputes, particularly with regards to adolescent dating. However, with a narcissistic dad, the degrading is extreme and massive during the teenage years.

This is particular to cases with idealization (doting on you, putting you on a platform). Maybe your dad showed friendship and care towards you when you were a little child since you were simpler to control, but later the delicate embrace directly after he got back home from work or the praising suddenly ended as you arrived at puberty. He wound up, facing an adolescent who was not as simple to maneuver.

For certain girls, affection was never a thing; the narcissistic dad would not touch, much less care for the daughter, and would ignore the little girl for the duration of her life.

Often, the narcissist picked one girl as a prodigy to put on the pedestal, while regarding the other daughter as the scapegoat or black sheep. Rarely he will talk with her and sometimes reaching the extreme point to disregard her existence.

With or without affection, the narcissistic dad's disregard for limits can become very upsetting. As certain daughters can confirm, becoming mindful of one's sexuality and starting relationships can be an immense 'trigger' for the father's desire to micromanage his youngsters.

Narcissistic fathers actually believe they own their kids entirely, and your expanding feeling of freedom can cause him narcissistic severe damage and anger.

To the narcissist dad, nobody is 'adequate' for his 'daughter' yet this conviction has much more profound and darker ramifications – he needs to guarantee that his girl remains in a condition of eternal youth with the goal that she is simpler to control.

Her interest in young men or young ladies is seen as a problem and propels him to enforce his authority and disgrace her in undesirable manners. He may have ingrained in the girl a dependency on his endorsement, which can be hard to remove.

A narcissistic father may have perpetrated secret incest that 'parentifies' the girl, so she develops the idea that only he could ever be her partner.

If the narcissist ever had a severe addiction, he may have her playing caretaker or more shockingly (if there's no mother around) a surrogate 'spouse' figure.

He may have subbed affection for financial 'liberality' and control, encouraging her that to be cherished, she needed likewise to be 'purchased' – and that, whoever purchased her, owned her.

On the other hand, if he had a son, he may have gloated about his sexual adventures and prowess teaching the boy to emulate him while setting a sexual double standard for his little girl, who he commands to remain 'unadulterated.'

There are numerous schemes for this type of sexual micromanaging, all of which will drain the kids' sense of independence and overall safety when growing up.

In worst-case scenarios, a dangerous narcissistic dad can even traverse to sexual maltreatment and brutality since they have no limits in the way they view their kids.

They consider them to be items to satisfy their needs, as expansions of themselves, as opposed to singular individuals.

By corrupting or degrading them explicitly, they keep up authority over the daughters through damaging schemes.

How to deal with this issue

Track the transition from idealization to devaluation. Was there a specific time your narcissist father quit idealizing you or was it just a consistent devaluation? Understanding the 'trigger point' can be useful to lessen the psychological disharmony that emerges when these kinds of dangerous people have raised us.

As we recognize the moment that we were devalued was the same moment we began to gain autonomy from the abusive parent, we comprehend that it was not our fault at all.

We may have felt embarrassed or even occupied with self-blame because of the maltreatment, without understanding that it had more to do with the narcissistic parent's inadequacies as opposed to any of our own apparent deficiencies.

Perceive flawed and negative input as tools to control you. It's imperative to start to break-down and reframe any feedback we get during such period as ill-conceived drivel intended to prevent us from discovering and becoming our real selves and from setting up relationships that would assist our journey into adulthood.

Supplant negative input and criticisms with more beneficial self-talk.

Take advantage of the power of positive declarations and affirmations, pattern intruding thoughts and practices that divert you from your inward critic, and rebuild the manners in which you've been addressing yourself. Take back your power.

Increase dominance over your body and sexual organization. As girls of narcissistic fathers, the sexuality may have been smothered, disintegrated, or abused to tender to the needs and desires of the narcissistic dad.

One of the ways is to get connected with a mystical sense of sexuality that empowers us to regard our sexuality as holy instead of a dishonorable practice of pleasure.

This is noteworthy in building relationships of well-being and trust.

It's all the more rewarding when working with an experienced trauma adviser who can assist you in disentangling any deeply rooted convictions or triggers that might be keeping you away from grasping your sexuality and discovering satisfaction in physical intimacy.

Narcissist fathers make a solid effort to keep up power and authority over their girls. It is vital that the girls of such parents take back their power, sexually, monetarily, emotionally, and mentally as they recuperate.

Since their narcissistic fathers formed the first plan for relationships, daughters of these fathers risk being stuck in a traumatic cycle and putting up with undesirable associations or companionship in adulthood.

Girls of narcissistic fathers may wind up being retraumatized by predators who are exactly the same as their primary male role models. This isn't to be blamed on them: anybody can become the main focus of a toxic narcissist without any consideration of their traumatic roots; also, anybody can be influenced by the impacts of traumatic experiences.

Lethal narcissistic sorts will, in general, locate a lot of narcissistic inventory in individuals who have sympathy, empathy, and assets, just as mental versatility developed from traumatic experiences.

The strength of survivors may, from the outset, appear to be an odd characteristic to comprehend in this specific circumstance. However, it is really one that the injurious narcissist relies upon in the maltreatment cycle.

Think about the fact that the offspring of narcissists might not have figured out how to execute fitting limits. However, they discovered how to endure while exposed to outrageous pressure.

These fundamental abilities of endurance may have been important in youth to stay away from the danger as well as physical mischief. However, in relationships, they become the very factors that can make us helpless to predators in adulthood.

The way Resilience plays its role in the trauma repetition cycle is the key factor to how daughters of narcissists who have been "built" for maltreatment may wind up experiencing one predator after another without deciphering the reason.

They blame themselves for keeping or getting into these relationships, not understanding that two of their most prominent qualities – the capacity to be versatile and their compassion for other people – are being used against them in a strategic maneuver.

Girls of narcissistic dads often become preys to be abused in adulthood since they are already used to being caretakers, adroit issue solvers and multi-taskers:

They figured out how to shuffle identifying dangers in their environment while reacting to them in such a way that relieved threat. They are amazingly equipped at carrying-out emotional work for others and getting on nonverbal prompts that could indicate risk or neglect.

An abusive relationship interprets this as "pleasing people." In a solid relationship, with limits and a desire for passionate correspondence, daughters of narcissists have a lot to offer their accomplices.

Their development, liberality, and mindfulness to their accomplice's needs can be resources in a healthy relationship after they have built up themselves with a firm sense of self.

However, in an oppressive one with a threatening narcissist, her ability to see her accomplice's point of view and address his issues gets exploited and utilized against her.

What might be astounding for people to comprehend is that it isn't only her weakness that makes her a target; her Resilience does as well.

This Resilience makes the daughter of a narcissistic father bounce back' after episodes of maltreatment and keep on attempting to fix the issues of the damaging relationship, just as she did in while young.

She will keep away from the dangers of encounter and strife, exposing her to the much more severe threat of being in a long and harmful relationship that exhausts and depletes her.

This is important to consider since narcissists will test the limits of their unfortunate victims ceaselessly all through the relationship to guarantee that the individual gets used to the maltreatment.

The most effective method to address this is to heal these subconscious injuries through mind and body procedures together with elective cures.

The subconscious personality really determines a lot of our conduct; that is the reason talk therapy by itself doesn't fix the considerable injury or profoundly damaging, instilled convictions.

It is likewise critical to understand that trauma is mostly stored in the body; its engraving is left on parts of the mind that don't have a lot of access to the more discerning pieces of our cerebrum and subsequently can't be mended 'intellectually.

That is the reason customary therapy must be added to EMDR. Hypnotherapy, trauma centered yoga, Reiki recuperating, fragrance-based treatment, sound bath treatment just as a day by day meditation practice, and exercise routine to 'purify' the subliminal wounds that might be tying them to these damaging accomplices or companions.

Have a sit-down with a psychological health professional to discover the treatments that best suit your triggers; understand that there is no all-encompassing recuperating way for survivors. What may work for one survivor may not be for you, yet as you try different things with various methods, you may very well discover the one for you.

Change the narratives and alter your conduct appropriately. Clinicians and sociologists state that we develop accounts out of our background to give our lives and personalities shape and significance. Bring any toxic accounts and convictions you have about yourself, your relationships, and the world to the surface – and disassemble them.

You may dismantle these through the recuperating methods we talked about, and you may likewise unravel these by digging into past systems of feeling, thinking, and characters.

How would you address yourself and take care of yourself every day? What kind of attitudes do you generally endure or overlook? How would you feel while exploring the globe? What is your story?

If you consistently engage with emotionally unavailable accomplices, for instance, this may be as a result of your youth trauma with emotionally unavailable people mainly from your father figure. You might have a background of feeling 'insufficient' and undeserving of a good relationship.

Find a way to supplant these stories with confirmations to recapture your sense of security just as your sacrosanct limits for future connections.

A more beneficial retelling of the account may look something like, "I am and consistently will be sufficient. Because I was traumatized doesn't mean I am to blame. I merit solid and safe relationships. I am a survivor, and I have it in me to change the narrative."

At that point, start to enforce and strengthen these new convictions and bond them by taking part in little moves that indicate that you're clearing another way to freedom.

For instance, restricting contact with narcissistic individuals can be a step to demonstrate to yourself that you are focused on your new conviction and that you can heed your gut feelings about harmful individuals.

Building a "consecrated boundary" list and conceptualizing a plan for executing more beneficial limits can likewise be useful to this procedure. For a rundown of rules for reasonableness and intimacy, have a look at the Human Bill of Rights by Pete Walker, the trauma therapist.

Look for good male role models. As a result of an abusive childhood, daughters of narcissist fathers tend to adopt the belief that men are dangerous or bankrupt emotionally.

This may become a channel by which they wind up meeting an ever-increasing number of risky men that certify this conviction about men and manliness. This is an attempt to heal the wounds of the past by reliving them.

In a world that is saturated with viciousness against the women — from rape to severe honor killings — it is possible that this feeling of danger has become part of the culture for some people.

The narrative that needs to change isn't about eradicating the legitimate dread of meeting toxic men but of welcoming the possibility of meeting safe men. They must know that 'safe' men still exist – men who do not purposely harm or threaten you.

These are the genuinely alluring and attractive men – regardless of whether your initial youth programming (which is no fault of yours) progressively attracts you to hazard.

Start paying attention to these men who offer you a whole new narrative – one of compassion and genuine love. Regardless of whether these good examples are celebrities as opposed to someone you really know, begin to consider the more liberal, gentler, and defensive guys you have either met or heard of.

Reach out – who knows? He might be your neighbor, your cohort, an educator who impacted you, a creator, a former sweetheart. The potential outcomes are unfathomable.

Consider the men who have once been in your life, who have endeavored to develop and have sincerely supported and approved you previously. By perceiving and comprehending more beneficial models, you can likewise discover the characteristics, attributes, and practices of what an emotionally available mate or companion would look and act like.

Though exposed to a past filled with complex trauma and redundancy, the daughters of narcissistic fathers can break free from this cycle. The will-power and perseverance of survivors can work well for them with regards to using the vital recuperating modalities, self-compassion, and resources required to mend themselves.

Notes:

_____

_____

_____

_____

_____

_____

_____

_____

_____

_____

_____

_____

_____

_____

_____

_____

_____

_____

_____

_____

_____

_____

_____

_____

Narcissistic Fathers

Narcissistic Fathers

Chapter 5: Narcissistic Father with their Sons

An absence of confidence drives sons of narcissistic dads. Groomed by an egotistical and presumptuous father, the ingrained low self-esteem prompts them to believe they are not sufficient to obtain their dad's endorsement.

The father might be controlling. He may put down and disgrace his child's missteps, helplessness, disappointments, or impediments, yet boast about him to his companions. He may flaunt about exaggerated accomplishments while demonizing those of his child.

A narcissistic father might bully and rival his child in games, mainly when the kid is a less-skilled. He might also be envious of the boy gains his spouse's attention, rival him, and flirt with his girlfriends or later spouse.

Narcissists show no empathy. Numerous narcissistic dads are dictators and inflexible about how things ought to be done (what they usually term as being a perfectionist) depicted by Robert Duval in the film The Great Santini.

"What I could never understand was your total lack of feeling for the shame and suffering you always inflict on me with your judgments" This letter from Franz Kafka to his father gives us a vivid painting of an imposing narcissistic father who is abusive and excessively egotistical.

His dictatorship decrees were passed on in a "repulsive and frightening tone filled with outrage and judgment. All those rules and decrees didn't apply to him, and this reality made them all the more discouraging to Franz Kafka.

Thus, Kafka couldn't be bold because all this had lowered his self-esteem. Like other offspring of narcissistic parents, he anticipated disgrace from his dad. He turned out to be so uncertain of everything in his life, including is very own body," inevitably prompting neuroses.

Once a narcissistic father engages with his son in any sport, he wants to dominate, oversee, and criticize. Often, narcissists are sticklers for perfection, so their sons are always below par, especially if you consider that they view their offspring to be expansions of themselves.

This makes them overly controlling, just like the father in the film Shine. On the other hand, narcissistic fathers are emotionally unavailable and are enveloped in their work and pleasures.

They consider duties like showing empathy to their son or showing up at their sons' basketball game to be insignificant and a considerable burden, despite the fact that they may accommodate him materially.

Since they deny and scorn their own reliance and helplessness, they take out all these insecurities on their sons and disgrace them at any indication of misery or shortcoming.

Franz Kafka experienced psychological mistreatment. He discloses that even though he once in a while got a flogged, its steady danger was the main problem, just as the blame and disgrace he suffered that always appeared as something he "merited." Some narcissistic fathers are physically coldblooded. One dad had his child cut the grass with a blade as a tool, and another dad made his child burrow a whole pool.

Abusive parents make a youngster develop a feeling of vulnerability, worthlessness, and powerlessness. As a grown-up, he may have continuous clashes with authority and control his outrage. This he turns on himself or others and gets forceful, passive-aggressive, or just passive.

Sons who don't become narcissistic fathers themselves experience the ill effects of codependency. They have been programmed to see themselves as somehow insufficient, a disturbance. Since they don't match their dad's desires, essentially, they are shameful even if their moms adore them; since kids need the love, affection, and acknowledgment of both their parents.

They're profoundly moved to get a conciliatory scrap of affection that others underestimate, as Franz discloses during his sicknesses. He couldn't control the tears when his dad showed up in his room only to investigate it and wave him. All

Franz Kafka remembered that he needed was just a little warmth, friendliness, and encouragement.

When growing up, maltreated youngsters figure out how to be independent and guarded. They resist being dependent, which prompts relationship issues. They may wed a narcissist or someone of the sort.

Sons of narcissistic fathers may be ambitious, but while trying to get the approval and endorsement of their dad, their prosperity feels empty. It's rarely ever enough even for them.

They have to teach themselves to be confident and set up limits in sound manners that are unknown and incomprehensible to them when growing up. They additionally need to esteem themselves and raise their confidence.

Many have experienced deep-rooted internal dejection because of the traumatic and abusive childhoods they experienced in their families. Nonetheless, recuperating and teaching them to acknowledge their identities and love themselves and also to get love is conceivable.

Notes:

_____

_____

_____

_____

_____

_____

_____

_____

_____

_____

_____

_____

_____

_____

_____

_____

_____

_____

_____

_____

_____

_____

_____

_____

_____

_____

Narcissistic Fathers

Chapter 6: Narcissistic Father Abuse on Adult Children

Children look up to their father specifically for strength and support. The patriarch role is so powerful that it easily bonds a child and his father for years. A loving father instills a great deal of self-esteem in his child from the way he cares, protects, and strengthens him/her.

Therefore, it becomes easy for a child to get attached to his father at a tender age. Emotional and mental attachment keeps most children in the dark about who their father is or why he behaves the way he does. Children find it hard to imagine that their father can be manipulative even when the traits are visible. Sometimes, a child might even feel guilty when their narcissistic dad resolves into physical violence. As a result, he/she carries the confused guilt around for the rest of his life. Narcissistic abuse from a father can vary from being mild to violent, depending on the extent of personality disorder in the father. Nevertheless, the abuse, no matter how small or significant, stay deep within the child's psychology for the rest of his life.

Narcissistic abuse from a father can affect a child's education. Since it affects the mind, the child struggles to make key decisions in life. The child is also exposed to substance abuse and addictions, as well as depression. All of these can remain with the child throughout his life.

Remember that the narcissistic dad needs to be in charge of everything and everyone. Therefore, he sets up his family against each other through manipulative approaches. The narcissistic dad has a personality disorder and so, lacks empathy. He can give gifts and mouth his love, but everything he does his for his personal gain. The narcissistic dad also wants to be the center of attention, and his children are one of his tools to achieve his aims.

Therefore, the narcissistic father, who is meant to protect his children, is now the source of the problems the child faces. A child that wishes to experience unconditional love is now exposed to violent and volatile narcissistic rage. He is now clouded in self-doubt from his father's open or subtle criticisms. He desires to be safe and secure in his biological home is now a fugitive, trying to run from his scheming and a self-centered, narcissistic father.

Here are some of the abuse a child faces from his narcissistic father.

Negative Criticism, Shaming or Bullying

For a narcissistic father, being on top is essential, and his children are the least of all people that would rise above them. Therefore, they need to gain control of their kids, most especially when he/she is now showing signs of independence. Shaming usually occurs at adolescence, which makes most children wonder what happened to the loving and caring dad when they were younger.

The narcissistic father uses negative criticism and shaming to destabilize the self-esteem of their daughter while they mainly use bullying to attack their son. This form of abuse cripples the child's sense of identity, and the primary purpose is to keep the child dependent on his father for as long as he pleases.

The narcissistic father criticizes his kids through comparison. He either compares the child with another golden child in the family or compares him/her with a perfect child in society. He abuses the child's academic, social, and professional performances if it does not measure with his own standards. To the narcissistic dad, the child is not another human being; he/she is only born as an extension of him. Therefore, the narcissistic father shames his child's mode of dressing or his choice of career. He mocks the type of friends and life goals of his child because it does not enhance his ego in any way.

As a result, the child is thrown into a state of an identity crisis. He finds it hard to know who he is or what he wants in life. The child goes through life working extra hard because he/she is trying to measure up with his father's standards.

Divisions Among Siblings

A narcissistic father desires to control people. Immediately he finds that his children are becoming difficult to control; he causes divisions among them. The ancient political strategy, 'divide and conquer,' is used to set siblings against themselves so that they can all depend on their father.

At first, this abuse comes like in like a little comparison like, 'why can't you be quiet like your sister.' The statement is subtle but very damaging because every child look up to their father and his validation means a lot to the children. The manipulative abuse becomes effective when it becomes glaring that one child is perfect while the other is flawed. The siblings go through life with this wrong self-centered validation without realizing the manipulation behind it.

The purpose of this psychological abuse is to keep siblings farther from each other. The narcissistic dad does this when he sees that his narcissistic supply is running low, and all attention is fading away from him when his kids love each other. This abuse is damaging to both the perfect and flawed child because they live with a false sense of self through life.

Using the Child to Enhance Self-Image

Like a man that moves around with a mirror, a narcissist is more concerned about his image in public. When he eventually has children, he uses them to improve his public image further. Therefore, a narcissistic dad must manage and gain control over his children. He must force them to think and act accordingly so that he can be valued in public. He must teach to walk or talk in a particular manner that reveals him to the world. This kind of abuse can be difficult to notice, especially when the father always showers his kids with gifts and spoken love. But, in reality, it is all a show.

This type of narcissistic abuse can be noticed in the way some men would brag about the academic performance of their son/daughter. They would subtly hint at their children's beauty and take them out on important public occasions. The love for their children is often emphasized publicly. However, inside, the child is pressured and criticized; he is like a slave who is taught and polished to be someone he is not.

This abuse from a narcissistic dad is common in popular high-achievers. Powerful public figures abuse their children by forcing a particular role on them. The child grows up as their father's pet, unable to grow beyond him and to try not to go below his expectations.

Infantilization

In the world of a narcissistic father, his children are always children. Even though they age, they are still his children. This narcissistic mindset leads to abuse that lingers even till adulthood. As a child grows, the narcissistic dad shifts from competition and control to intrusion. He goes from shaming his child to crossing boundaries without seeking approval.

This abusive tendency makes it difficult for the child to make key decisions, and the abuse is prevalent in golden children. It is easier for a scapegoat to take his stance against this form of violence than it is for the perfect kid. The golden child will have to rethink his respect for his narcissistic father now that he is growing and needs some space away from home.

Sexual Bully

People with Personality Disorders are never consistent; it is even worse with Narcissistic Personality disorder. A Narcissist is obsessive about himself, and this extends to his children, which he sees as a mere extension of himself. As a result, he results in a sexual bully when he sees that his child is developing visible sexual organs.

The narcissistic dad sees his growing male child as a competition while he sees his growing daughter as a threat to his narcissistic supply. Eventually, he uses Sexual bullying to control his children. Sexual bullying can be in the form of not informing the child about Sex and his changing bodies. Sometimes, the narcissistic fathers threaten his son/daughter about dating someone or having sex. Other times, the narcissistic dad intrudes on the privacy by demanding to know everything about their boyfriends and girlfriends. In worse cases, some fathers sexually abuse their children by demanding to see their bodies.

Sex is a very sensitive issue for many adolescences. Therefore, this psychological abuse can affect the child for a very long time. A child that is used to sexual bullying is exposed to anger, hatred, and addictions.

Neglect

Ignoring narcissistic fathers easily neglect their children. This is not out of a specific hatred; covert narcissistic cannot merely show empathy. They are often cold and dismissive. A child that has gone through neglect also finds it difficult to show empathy. Most times, they become narcissists like their father.

A narcissistic father neglects his child by being inattentive to the child's needs. His only obligation to the child is to help him gain moral grounds in public. He employs a caregiver for his child and might not even touch the child throughout his growth

This kind of abuse is from a narcissistic father that is extremely obsessed with himself. Even though he does not intrude on his child's privacy, he is basically not there at all to even know the child or give moral and mental support. Most children that experience this kind of abuse are exposed to different personality disorders like NPD. The child goes through life in search of fatherly love and becomes envious of others who had such love.

Parentification

Every narcissist is self-centered. Unfortunately, this will not change when they marry and have children; it will not change when they are aging. The illusion most children chase is that the narcissistic father will eventually slow down, rethink, and change his behaviors. This does not always happen.

Therefore, using this illusion, the aging narcissistic father 'parentifies' his children. He places unfair parental responsibilities on his child while he sits back and does nothing. Sometimes, he uses pleas, apologies, and emotional blackmail to manipulate his child into abandoning their lives for him.

Parentification abuse can make an adult child of a narcissistic lose out on so many things like relationship, finance, and career. In the child's mind, he is obligated to help his toxic father, and there is also a possibility for change. This is false because the narcissistic father will use this opportunity to further intrude on his child's privacy and mess up key areas of his child's life.

Gaslighting

Gaslighting is a common term used in the world of narcissism. It is commonly used by the narcissist to boost their ego, and by many parents unwittingly to control their kids. Narcissistic father use gaslighting to shame their growing children.

Gaslighting is a way of distorting reality. Whenever a child perceives that something is not right, he/she is immediately put off the thought by a gaslighting reaction. For instance, when a child sees that his father is wrong, he/she is immediately reminded of his age and experience. A narcissistic dad would never argue with his child based on facts. He will leave the events and attack the child's personality and mistakes; he will make a subtle remark about his experience and how he is right merely because he is the father. This is gaslighting.

A child that is exposed to this abuse is always confused and unsure of himself. The child is often critical of a different opinion as he is not certain of his own opinion.

Notes:

Chapter 7: The Narcissistic Enabler: Wife of the Narcissistic Father

There is always somebody backing the narcissist. Being, in a general sense, dependent on others for the confidence they need, narcissists don't get much of anything without having their influencers, someone that cheers them on. The enabler underpins the narcissist's overwhelming persona, the extraordinary feeling of privilege, and oppressive conduct by undeniably tolerating his adaptation of the real world, not confronting his maltreatment, covering up or tidying up his wrecks, and going about as a theological rationalist for him.

This enabler can be exceptionally kind, is horribly faithful to the narcissist, and has an extraordinary measure of sympathy for the harmed individual that he is. So they ignore the narcissist's conduct, apologize to everyone for their maltreatment, and make light of the maltreatments due to fear of being attacked by the narcissist.

Narcissistic dads, for the most part, have these empowering influences in their family. As a rule, the Wife assumes that job. They may likewise have empowering companions, collaborators or representatives, and different individuals from their informal community. Individuals become empowering influences of narcissists for various reasons, from misinformed care-taking to self-question, to fear, to a craving for control. Regularly they become empowering influences steadily without realizing their circumstances. A narcissist's accomplice, the Wife, in this case, may feel confounded by that accomplice's indoctrinating messages, trusting a few or the entirety of the accompanying:

The empowering influence regularly feels dependent on the narcissist, detached in their maltreatment, and just as they are going insane. We should not overlook that in the entirety of this wreckage, the empowering influence has likewise been unbelievably rationally harmed, controlled, and mentally conditioned by the narcissist. Now and again, they shut down.

The Wrong Mindset of the Wife

The spouse of the narcissistic man thinks her decisions made him act rashly. "I am uncalled for one. On the off chance that I wasn't so narrow-minded or ugly, he would adore me." She feels her significant other doesn't generally mean to hurt her or the children. She accepts the narcissistic man she had remained with for her entire life adores her, and the kids, however, don't have the foggiest idea how to show it. "All connections are troublesome like this," she murmurs. "Things will show signs of improvement when we get hitched and have children. If I change, he will be content with me. On the off chance that I am all the more adoring, he will quit acting so furious. On the off chance that our kids carried on well, he will be content with us."

As a rule, the spouse of the narcissistic man considers damaging to be seeing someone typical because they grew up with requesting, narrow-minded, careless, or injurious guardians. Empowering influences of narcissists may originate from narcissistic homes or different conditions in which they figured out how to enslave their needs and sentiments, for example, in support of a drunkard or a rationally sick parent.

She may swindle herself into feeling that only she can comprehend and satisfy the troublesome yet exceptional accomplice. She may consider her to be as by one way or another an incredible catch and accept she needs to do additional work to keep him. Maybe her significant other gets a handle on a touch of her alliance—progressively insightful, gorgeous, enchanting, instructed, rich, or fruitful than her and along these lines worth the great support she needs to do. Mostly, a narcissistic father's prodigy might be under the daydream that s/he is the one in particular who can deal with that parent's bliss. Such kids regularly build their personality around the requests of the parent, continually attempting to please and conciliate.

The empowering spouse of a narcissistic husband is likewise character confused, and the truth is told, an optional abuser since she keeps her kid in a flat out the dungeon. The disappointment of the parent to help the youngster when in urgent need of discharge from the narcissistic circumstance recommends that the empowering guardian's needs mean more to the parent than the necessities of the kid.

The dismal reality about empowering influences' is that many empowering guardians are in established truth, the kinder parent to the substitute kid, and to different kids too. Be that as it may, the positive empowering influence is a diverse assortment; and now and again, this parent can be absolute loathsome to their kids.

Empowering spouses will, in general, anticipate that help from the kids should contain the troublesome circumstance and the narcissist's anger. They expect that the youngster should satisfy the narcissist, to keep them content, and to ensure the narcissist feels appreciated, unique, and thought about constantly. In the circumstances, for example, these, she will sustain the maltreatment by having abnormally high requirements of the youngster; and will anticipate that the kid should show the narcissist the most extreme regard, in any event, when the narcissist isn't regarding the kid.

The spouse of a narcissistic man won't meet the kid without anyone else enthusiastic level, approve the kid, and leave the narcissist.

Why an Enabling Wife is likewise a Narcissist

As often as possible, empowering spouses of narcissists remain in their connections in any event, when they understand they are being maltreated because they don't see an exit plan. Their damaging spouse is probably going to have undermined her freedom. He could encourage a group of people by dissolving her fearlessness, troubling her with unreasonable obligations and issues, separating her from loved ones, depleting her accounts, distancing her from their youngsters, and taking steps to leave her with nothing.

Now and again, an empowering influence might be a clandestine narcissist dazzled with the obvious certainty or accomplishment of an increasingly clear narcissist. Such an empowering spouse may appreciate the other narcissist and feed her confidence and personality by living vicariously through her significant other. Or on the other hand, the more hidden narcissistic spouse may determine fulfillment and social consideration and endorsement from dealing with the obvious narcissist's troublesome and narrow-minded character. In such a relationship, the narcissistic empowering spouse may introduce herself as the forbearing great, kind, steadfast, persistent unfortunate casualty who merits better; however, beneath the surface is similarly as exploitive and controlling as her significant other. As it were the narcissist spouse empowers the undercover Wife through positive or negative affiliation. As guardians, both narcissistic accomplices empower each other by ignoring as well as supporting their careless and harsh conduct toward their kids.

How the relationship is fortified

Regularly a narcissist man controls his significant other through rotating misuse and unique treatment. The empowering spouse falls into an example of staying away from assault while additionally looking for remunerations, for instance, warmth, applause, sex, or cash. In this powerful, the spouse encounters injury holding with the damaging narcissistic man, turning out to be sincerely and physically dependent on the thrill ride of positive and negative fortification.

The empowering spouse panders to the narcissist, attempts to keep them glad, and will even turn into a piece of the maltreatment of the youngsters if it implies the narcissist will ease up. Toward the day's end, they are the narcissist's sidekick, an officer in the narcissist's military, and completely propagate the harassing plague much further.

A ton of ladies makes light of the maltreatment from their narcissistic spouse. They advise the kids to toughen up and to pardon the narcissist. This reality addresses the empowering agent's capacity to get to genuine compassion. Is the empowering influence really compassionate by any means? All things considered, while their kid is being slandered, the empowering agent watches, says 'don't be so touchy presently, forgive and never look back,' and progresses forward.

What keeps the empowering influence in the home with the narcissist?

The empowering spouse is the ideal injured individual for the narcissistic man. She is regularly calm, simple to converse with, exceptionally tranquil, and seems to have a great deal of sympathy. She likewise needs certainty, re-think themselves, doesn't tune in to their gut, and don't put stock in themselves. Be that as it may, three central point keeps her with her narcissistic spouse.

Religion:

There is an assortment of reasons for why an empowering influence would need to remain in a long-lasting marriage with a toxic man. For some, it is the fear of religion. They accept that they are not permitted to leave their accomplice, and once wedded to a purported Christian narcissist, the

Wife, paying little heed to kids or not, must do all that they can to keep up the relationship.

Intergenerational designs:

The empowering influence might be carrying on family designs. They may have had an empowering guardian, and a narcissistic parent.

Dread:

The empowering agent may accept that there is no reason for leaving supposing that they do go, the narcissist will make their life a horrific experience.

Solace:

Some empowering influences' are not worried about the maltreatment of the kids and are glad to remain with an abuser for their solace delights.

The Wife's job as "Flying Monkeys."

The empowering spouse is stuck with the narcissistic dad and their youngsters. They enable terrible psychological mistreatment to happen and become a flying monkey to the narcissist as opposed to supporting the youngster.

"Flying monkeys" are empowering agents who additionally execute the narcissist's maltreatment on focused unfortunate casualties. The term is utilized in the Disney film, "The Wizard of Oz." A spouse that is progressively associated with the narcissistic man acts like a "Flying Monkey" by helping him to do his dirty work and complete maltreatment as a substitute. There is a scarce difference between a spouse going about as an empowering influence and going about as a flying monkey. Regularly the spouses go too far to abstain from being focused on themselves or because they are put resources into accepting the falsehoods that legitimize the narcissist's maltreatment of others, especially scapegoated kids. For such youngsters, the double-crossing of the empowering spouse might be more diligently to acknowledge and excuse than that of the narcissist because the empowering influence is the "protected" parent who should know better.

The Scapegoat and the spouse of his narcissistic father

In adulthood, the Scapegoat doesn't have a clue how to feel about the empowering spouse. They realize that their mom seemed to think about them more than the narcissist, and even endeavored to shield them from severe maltreatment now and again. Nonetheless, in the Scapegoat's eyes, the empowering influence didn't do what's needed; and a significant part of the time, picking up help from his/her mom resembled playing a round of lotto. It might occur, or it may not. Backing from empowering spouses can regularly rely upon their feelings at the time.

For the substitute, the situation goes something like this: the spouse may bolster them today when the narcissist considers them a 'bitch' for reasons unknown, or they may not.

The spouse improves the substitute's dread that they are insane. Rather than approving the kid, and disclosing to them they are not the insane one, they regularly unknowingly bolster the narcissist father by safeguarding their debilitated impression of the substitute, which isn't genuine, was rarely pure, and will never be authentic.

A kid needs to adore his parents. They paid for the tuition-based school expenses, arrange props, dental arrangements, and swimming exercises; things that generally would undoubtedly not have occurred if the youngster was left in the narcissist's consideration without the empowering spouse. They need to adore their mother, who frequently requested that the narcissist quit calling the youngster names, embraced and held the kid, disclosed to them they cherished them, and appeared to esteem this kid to a great extent sincerely.

Nonetheless, the passionate clash that the substitute youngster experiences in connection to the empowering guardian are unadulterated mental anguish since, indeed, his/her mother truly was the main adoring guardian to the kid, this is valid.

Where it turns out to be mind-boggling for kids, and their empowering mother is that she is regularly the kindest parent, the most tranquil, and the motivation behind why the narcissist didn't conclusively demolish the youngster. The empowering spouse indicated the youngster some affection, which might just be the explanation they turned out the opposite side. Be that as it may, this parent is likewise the motivation behind why the kid got devastated from multiple points of view and now battles appallingly in adulthood.

The substitute's general examination of the empowering agent is that they were a piece of the maltreatment and did an inappropriate thing.

Notes:

_____
_____
_____
_____
_____
_____
_____
_____
_____
_____
_____
_____
_____
_____
_____
_____
_____
_____
_____
_____
_____
_____
_____
_____
_____
_____

Narcissistic Fathers

Chapter 8: Test to Recognize a Narcissistic Father

You might be wondering if your father is a narcissist or not. Ask yourself the following questions to recognize if your mother is a narcissist. I decided to avoid any final ranking or score. The purpose of the test is to allow you to take some time to think, preferably in a quiet place, and to talk with yourself. The answer will come. It is there, in some hidden part of your heart.

Does Your father hate taking responsibility?

One of the telltale signs of a narcissist is that they do not like taking responsibility. As a result, even when they are wrong, they have some tactics

173

to prevent the blame. Hence, you might consider the blame for some things your father did while growing up.

The idea is simple, and you were an easy prey less likely to object or argue. In addition, you wanted to protect your father. This is the instinct present in all kids and parents.

Does Your father lack the Right Emotions?

Careful consideration of the life of a narcissist reveals that everything about them centers on them alone. As a result, they cannot feel appropriate emotions. In other words, your father is neither capable of love nor capable of expressing any tangible emotions like regrets.

As a result, when they do something wrong, apology, and asking for forgiveness is not is their dictionary. They continue life as if nothing happens, even after hurting people intentionally.

Does Your father like bragging?

They brag about everything. The conspicuous ones make it distinct and express it in the form of exaggeration while it could be insidious as well. Their achievements mean a lot to them, and they care about it more than anything else in the world. As a result, they are always talking about it.

Does Your father Lie to You?

One of the telltale signs of a narcissist is lying. This is one of their weapons of manipulations to get what they want from people. Unfortunately, they lie to themselves as well. As a result, your father might be fond of blowing his own trumpet and even exaggerating his importance in a bid to look better before friends and families.

Narcissists, however, know when they are lying. They differ from compulsive liars that do not understand the meaning of lying.

Does Your Father Manipulate You?

One of the weapons in the arsenal of a narcissist is manipulation. Manipulation is one of the weapons that allow them to gain control of others and their children.

For instance, your dad might find pleasure comparing you to another of your siblings. He might shame you, embarrass you or nag you when you do not comply with his biddings. He might even say you are a bad kid all because he wants to have his way with you!

Does the Use Comparison as a Weapon?

Does your father never stop talking about something beautiful someone eels did all in an aim to make you feel bad for not doing the same thing up to standard? He is likely a narcissist. Without uttering a word, he expresses his disdain and complements you sarcastically in an insincere and unjust manner.

He Sees Nothing Wrong Violating Your Boundary

In other words, you always feel you are a continuation of your father. He finds it easy taking your property and giving them out without excuse. When you confront an object, daddy says he bought them for you; hence they were never yours. He finds it easy taking your time without caring about what you have to do.

Your privacy means nothing to daddy as he sees nothing wrong storming into your bedroom or bathroom without knocking. He asks snoops into your personal life, reads your diary, emails, and even checks your chat. Daddy likes digging into your feelings and keeps looking for things (mainly negative) that can be used against you.

Does Daddy Undermine You?

In other words, nothing you do can ever please him. The only time he will acknowledge your accomplishments is if he can take credit for them. If it doesn't benefit him, he ignores them or belittles the achievement!

Since he can't be the center of attention, he passes negative or derogatory remarks. He leaves the occasion early and acts like it is of no importance.

Does Daddy Use Codependency to Control you?

There are times kids feel like they cannot live without their parents. This is because, over the years, daddy has planted the feeling that they cannot live without them, which affects them. Even though most parents want their kids to be with them for as long as possible, they know it is not possible.

Since a narcissist always has to be in control, they do everything to keep you closer. They are never proud of a critical moment and fantastic milestones you achieve, like landing your first job or getting married. They know this will make you leave them, which means their control over you is over!

Does Daddy hate Criticism?

A narcissist derives pleasure in making jest of someone. They, however, do not like it when people do the same to them. This is because Criticism makes daddy feel inadequate and less of himself, which is unacceptable to him.

Is Daddy Always Envious?

In other words, daddy always loves to be the center of attention. This means whatever you do, it will never impress your daddy. As a result, when you get something right or do something worth being proud of, daddy will be envious and jealous. He might even make an effort to spoil it for you or try to be in the spotlight.

Does Daddy Likes Toil with Your Emotions?

In other words, whatever causes you pain pleases daddy. This is a sick and typical behavior among narcissists. They use a concept known as sadism to feed on their children's emotions. He finds pleasure in doing things to hurt you. He goes over a cycle of teasing and praising all in a bid to bring out the worst in you.

Is Daddy Willful and Selfish?

A healthy and sane parent will want the best for their kids, not a narcissistic father. They are always after the best of everything. He takes pride in following his ways and will follow it without caring what it will cost him, his kids, or others around him.

Daddy will go to extreme length to have what you objected to, even if you were right about not giving him or he demanded it selfishly.

Does Daddy Lacks Insight?

Since a narcissist's emotion is not developed, they do not know how to engage with people. As a result, they shy away from responsibility in all situations. To a narcissist father, he believes that the best and only way to handle a situation is that you and mummy meet his need, nothing else. This takes priority in all his relationships with people.

Does Daddy Pretend to Listen?

While daddy might even pretend to be a good listener, he is not. In reality, daddy is looking for things or what he can use against you in al conversation. He is on the watch out to discredit you. To daddy, he needs to criticize and judge you to fulfill his ego.

Does Daddy Exaggerate?

Daddy has a unique and devilish way of turning things around and manipulating the truth so that it favors him. Even when you realize and catches the lie, he has a particular form of sugarcoating everything in a manner to confuse you. This makes you wonder if whether you or daddy is right!

Is Daddy Always Loud?

Daddy likes talking louder because it makes it seem smart and serious before other people. This is daddy's habit as he does not even mind to embarrass you and the entire family in public.

Daddy's loud voice is a tactic to cajole you or anyone else into submitting. Bear in mind, however, that you should never have a shouting contest with daddy as you will not win!

Is Daddy Always Negative?

When you genuinely try to understand a narcissistic father, you will discover that happiness is far from him. This is evident in their behavior and character. It also explains why daddy likes yelling and screaming at people.

Happiness is far from daddy, and it is his delight to make everyone around him miserable, including his kids. Getting other people angry makes them happy and in control, because it gives them the confirmation of being in control.

Does Daddy Ridicule You

Whatever you do or accomplish, daddy will always find a way to make you feel miserable about it. He is so skilled that no one but you and daddy will not see the manipulation. It might be as simple as scolding you in public. Yet, hidden underneath that insidious act is a plot to hurt and ridicule you.

Does Daddy Make you doubt yourself?

Whatever is important to you does not interest daddy as long as he gains nothing from it. In other words, daddy will make you feel bad for doing and saying things that mean no harm. Your efforts are worthless and never enough since daddy does not care. Daddy also does not care about your feelings; hence you are irrelevant.

Does Daddy Ignore Your problems?

A healthy parent will do anything to help their kids solve any problem. It is not the same as a narcissistic father. Empathy is not in their dictionary; hence should you have any problem, they find a way of making it personal. They will come up with something similar but horrible, all in a bid of getting the spotlight off you.

If you quarreled with a friend or sibling, for instance, daddy has a way of turning things around. He will make you look and feel bad. He does not care about how you feel or whether you are hurt, so ignoring your problem means nothing.

Is Daddy Oblivious?

A narcissist does not know and accepts that he is broken. As a result, daddy does not know the effect of his actions and behaviors on you and others around him. This is one of the reasons why getting a narcissist to seek help is really stressful and challenging.

As a result, daddy is incapable of developing a healthy relationship with you and other people. In all their interactions, they like being the center of attention. This makes it difficult for daddy to have any reasonable and meaningful two-way relationship with you and others.

Does Daddy Like Shaming You?

A narcissist father is always shaming his children. This is in a bid to wear off their self-confidence and make sure they never develop their self-esteem. This is because daddy is trying to make sure you are not mature and advanced to the extent of living independently.

Daddy does not have any issue shaming you or passing derogatory remarks about you to others. Your achievements academically, career-wise, and socially mean nothing to daddy.

Conclusion

This chapter has shed light extensively on the proven steps and tests to know and determine if your father is a narcissist. When you consider some of the above points, and it describes the personality of your father, there is a significant probability that he is a narcissist.

Notes:

_____
_____
_____
_____
_____
_____
_____
_____
_____
_____
_____
_____
_____
_____
_____
_____
_____
_____
_____
_____
_____
_____
_____
_____
_____
_____
_____

Narcissistic Fathers

Chapter 9: The Golden Child and Scapegoat Concept

The Scapegoat Syndrome

In some cultures, and even the Christian religion, a goat was chosen to bear the sin of the whole community and let loose into the wide. This was a practice to appease the gods then. When the animal is cast out, the community assumes it is clean and free from all wrongdoings.

The concept of scapegoating since then has found applications in towns, communities, families, and nations. A scapegoat takes the fall for wrongdoing and is usually punished. This same process happens in families.

In families, a scapegoat might be a temporary role and could rotate between a different child in the family.

Alternating the Fall Guy

With a controlling father, the role of a scapegoat can be adopted in a family. The father is often strict and a perfectionist. In his world, everything is either right or wrong, with no middle ground or compromise. If things go out of hand, there must be someone to take the fall, as well as a reason. Do not expect daddy to take the fall as a narcissist is never wrong (in their world).

As a result, when the kids leave the window opened, and rainwater splashed in, either Jessica or Kyle must take responsibility. The narcissistic father, being controlling in nature, must have a reason for bad things to happen and someone to bear it.

Since the children now know that someone will take the blame regardless of what happens, siblings will be on each other's throat. They will all be fighting hard to get on daddy's good side.

As part of their means to avoid taking the fall, they resort to the blame game.

A disturbed father also uses the revolving scapegoat to maintain control over his children. He also uses it to remind himself that he is doing a terrific job. In his world, he is not a bully and a dictator, but a strict father with authority who does not mind seeing his kid follow the path he has set for them.

The permanent scapegoat

There are situations when the parent assigns the permanent scapegoat. This makes other kids think of themselves as healthy, perfect, and more likable. This is so as they do not take responsibility for their actions. The father makes them believe that the presence of the child (scapegoat) is a curse to the family. He assumes that if he could fix the kid or get him/her to behave normal, life will be better.

The permanent scapegoat assumes responsibility for every wrongdoing in the family. Whenever there is a deviation from what the father assumes as a perfect family, he already has a set explanation. All the family members do not consider the parenting skill of their fathers. Instead, the laser is beamed in the unfortunate kid who is always messing things up.

Since there is a scapegoat always to take the fall, nobody cares about how the father runs the family or the interaction between the family members. The presence of the scapegoat keeps the father above all blame and reproach.

Effect of Scapegoating on the Child

Every kid that is unfortunate to be scapegoated does develop a thick emotional skin. Many at times, they know they are being bullied and mistreated. They are aware of the unfair treatment, and the culmination of the whole experience does not leave them.

It could prompt them to be high achievers where they see themselves working hard to prove their father wrong. This might be good in a sense. On the other hand, as well, they might have absorbed, internalize, and accepted all the horrible and negative comments from their father such that do nothing. In either way, they sustain both physiological and emotional wounds.

The bright side of all this, however, is the fact that it is the scapegoated kid, out of all the children of the narcissistic parent, that likely knows his father for who he really is.

In other words, the child can see the toxic behavioral pattern of her dad and other siblings.

Not only that, since he/she suffers most, he/she is likely to get help in the form of healing from the effect of the toxic relationship with the father and siblings.

Scapegoating on other Children: The Effect

We can liken the children of a narcissistic father to planets in their orbits. Even with the mother still, as the sun (the center of attention), the father uses the same tactics on the kids. To a narcissistic father, the children are an extension of himself, well except the rejected and scapegoated one, of course. As a result of this, the status of the kid changes in time. This brings us to the concept of the golden child, also known as the trophy child, that is a perfect reflection of the mother. The child is more like daddy and even high in narcissistic traits. The narcissistic world is not governed by rational human logic. It depends on how good you can impress your mother. It does not revolve around character or empathy. This leads us to the concept of the golden child.

Conclusion

Not infrequently, the "scapegoat" is the first to leave the family. This happens not following a physiological and healthy process of release from the family of origin, but following a maneuver of expulsion from the nucleus that forces the child to flee.

The Golden Child Syndrome

The Golden child does not understand the concept of introspection and self. To the child, love is conditional and transactional. (You only have my love and approval when you do well for me.) Sadly, however, the child will likely carry this

194

faulty mentality to adulthood. Still hanging on to what transpired in the family when they were kids, he's more likely to grow up to become a narcissist.

The child is clueless and not aware of how the narcissist father has affected him. He is clueless about how devoid of empathy he is. This is not a true recipe for happiness and love.

Before examining the concept of the golden child in detail, it is essential to note that every parent dreams of one before they know how to make one. It is normal for parents to want their kids to have access to the best of the best. All parents, healthy parents, at that, have the best interest of their kids at heart. This explains why they provide them with the best resources to make life easy for them.

In a family, however, that any of the parents show signs of narcissistic tendencies, the dynamics are affected severely.

How to Know the Golden Child of a Family

In a healthy and productive family structure, the parents are balanced and secured. They know how to create a healthy environment for their kids. They know how to foster self-development and ensure a productive environment. Also, they know how to keep their parents within limits without being too toxic on them.

Healthy and normal parents rely on empathy, transparency, and understanding to create a healthy bond with their kids. They do not use Criticism, guilt, shame, and other diabolic manipulation technique to create insecure, broken, and anxious kids.

If you understand a narcissist, you should know they have no real sense of self. Their sense-of-being revolves around an idealized self that needs constant feeding to keep up with.

In a family, when any of the parents is a narcissist, the kids become a narcissistic supply to feed them and keep their personality intact. In other words, they do not really nurture a healthy child and create a healthy environment for them. Instead, they create an environment in which the kid's image revolves around satisfying the parents and the child sacrificing their personality for the parents.

The child does not have a distinct sense of self as their boundaries are interwoven with the kids. This forms the basic foundation of the golden child. In short, she/he is an extension of the narcissist parent – the father in this case.

Bear in mind that part of the distinct personality of a narcissist is that they can never be wrong. They are perfect and above everyone. In the same manner, the golden child is that special and unique kid that is an extension of their perfect and distinct characters. This explains why a golden child always move about with the impression that he/she is special

Now that we have established how a golden child comes into being, the next section explores the distinct characters of a golden child within a narcissistic family.

She/he is competitive

Since a golden child is an extension of their narcissistic parent, they are bound to reflect their competitive nature. As a result, the child is always striving with the siblings. The narcissistic family, being dysfunctional, also encourages competition.

As a result, the child and other family members grow up being competitive in nature.

They do not mind taking a risk and going against morals to ensure they are the most preferred in every area of life. They depend on external sources for reinforcement to boost their self-esteem and self-confidence.

The child love Studying

There is a significant probability that the golden child will devote more time to studying. Bear in mind that it is in their nature to be competitive. This explains why they love studying, going to school, and taking part in competitive events.

What other place provides the best place for them to be competitive than school. They love going to school and thrive in competitions. They are celebrated in the class as they find it easy to get on the right sides of their teachers as well.

They are the Obedient Child

Children generally are rebellious by nature. They revolt to authority and, by default, do not like it when controlled. To a golden child, however, this is not so. Their parents are their deity, and they obey their rules and dictates to the letter.

They do not talk back to their parents. They do not question their decision, and they do not mind giving up their needs as long as their parents are satisfied.

They have productive Hobbies

You will hardly find a golden child playing video games and computer games. Instead, they prefer to dedicate themselves to satisfying and inspiring hobbies. As a result, they are continually improving.

They prefer devoting their time to books, learning an instrument or a foreign language. They will likely pick up a hobby, like painting and sports.

He/she is sensitive to Criticism

The golden child knows that he is special. They know that they have a unique DNA that sets them apart from the pack (even though this is false.) They manifest this in their character by holding themselves in high esteem and carrying themselves with grace and vigor.

This is why they do not take Criticism lightly. Correcting or criticizing their effort does not go down well with them.

The child Seeks perfection

Even at a tender age, the golden child has been brought up in perfection. They must be neat and tidy and their clothes without blemish. Their food must be perfect and seasoned the way they want it. Their room must be neat and always organized. They do not settle for anything less than a distinction in their studies.

They punish and beat themselves up when they fail. When they do not meet up to expectations, they will beat themselves up for days. The golden child meets the description of the perfect child. This is the dream child of all mothers.

The problem, however, is that many fail to see fragility and emptiness behind this supposed perfection. They live with this illusion until they grow up, and their world becomes disoriented when they fail reality.

Conclusion

The development of a golden child is marred as they are sick emotionally and psychologically. As a result, when these kids grow up, finding their real self and identity becomes a problem.

When they eventually survive the ordeal of growing up, taking care of themselves, making their decisions, and standing up for themselves becomes a problem. As perfect, nice, and appealing a golden child seems, this is their flaw.

Thank you again for choosing Narcissistic Fathers. I hope you will find it. I would like to hear your thoughts with a short review on Amazon

Notes:

_____

_____

_____

_____

_____

_____

_____

_____

_____

_____

_____

_____

_____

_____

_____

_____

_____

_____

_____

_____

_____

_____

_____

_____

Narcissistic Fathers

Narcissistic Fathers

PART THREE: RECOVERING FROM A NARCISSISTIC MOTHER

Chapter 1: Handling your Narcissistic Father

Since you have understood that your dad is a run of the mill narcissist. How might you handle them with the data you have. They might be bad-to-the-bone, with Narcissistic Personality Disorder (NPD), they may have narcissistic attributes, or they might be a mind-boggling assortment of guardians, stepparents, as well as parental figures who fall in different places along the narcissism continuum. Whatever the fact of the matter is in your group of the starting point and anyway old you will be, you have to push ahead with your very own life. It's rarely past the point of no return or too soon to define limits, process your emotions, and work on mending. Regardless of whether you are a minor as yet living at home, there are numerous ways you can support yourself. On the off chance that a narcissistic dad raised you, here are steps you can take right now on your mending way.

Pick up everything about NPD (Narcissistic Personality Disorder)

In case you're new to the acknowledgment that your dad is a narcissist, you have to continue finding out about what you're managing. Quest the Internet for good assets. Peruse and join talk gatherings like Psychforums and Survivors forum. Watch motion pictures and shows with narcissistic characters, discover a specialist who gets narcissism. The more you teach yourself and discover support, the more you will comprehend what you've experienced and what you have to do to move past the lethal impact of your family.

Your Narcissistic Father Will Not Change; Don't Chase the Illusion

One of the most troublesome difficulties you face is tolerating that your narcissist father more than likely will never show signs of change. If the narcissist in your life figures out how to gain individual ground toward a more advantageous condition of being extraordinary, yet you ought to expect he won't. Narcissistic dads once in a while change, and on the off chance that they are acting more pleasant, it is probably a manipulative move. Holding out the expectation that your father will, at last, give you the unqualified love you have hungered for as long as you can remember, is normal. However, it is a bogus dream that makes you powerless against further misuse and prevents you from proceeding onward.

Perceive the Role Your Mother Played

Where there is a narcissistic dad, there will be an empowering mother; if not, they would have separated. What does that truly mean? By obliging or pardoning the narcissist's harsh conduct, your empowering mother basically "standardize" and continue it. In some cases, your mom additionally goes about as "flying monkeys" by helping her narcissist spouse in his dirty work, overlooking and propagating her maltreatment. By not naming the maltreatment and not shielding her children from it, empowering spouses to become complicit, regardless of whether they are additionally exploited by it.

Now and then sympathetic, the empowering mother can be as hard or harder than excusing your dangerous dad. Individuals with NPD have a character issue shaped in early youth by a staggering hardship. Even though the narcissistic man may act immensely, you may wind up feeling more terrible about the more practical empowering lady. You may ask why she pardoned the narcissist and didn't shield you from misuse, and you may feel horrendously sold out by her complicity.

Which role Did you Play?

Is it true that you were a substitute or the prodigy? Have you acted now and again as a flying monkey? Jobs are regularly liquid in the narcissistic family, contingent upon your father's plan. Maybe you have been the prodigy and scapegoated. Since the narcissist father keeps up control by making divisions (separate and overcome) among relatives, you may feel estranged from your other parent and kin. Maybe you feel double-crossed by them. Remember that every one of you has been a piece of a twisted framework organized by the predominant narcissist father in the family uniquely to serve his needs to the detriment of others. In a certain way, you have all been battling to make do with the role you have been thrown in.

The most dominant guard against a narcissist man is a bound together front. If you can discover common comprehension and solidarity with your other relatives, that can be an enabling method to close down the narcissist's maltreatment, just as a significant wellspring of approval for what you have experienced. Nevertheless, if your mom is not dependable or open to discussing the narcissism in your family, you need most importantly to ensure yourself and point of confinement contact with everybody.

With regards to Boundaries, Be Strict

Narcissists always abuse limits. They see others, especially their youngsters, as augmentations of themselves to control. As the prodigy, your responsibility is to reflect what your dad desire to find in himself and wishes to extend to the world. As a substitute, your primary responsibility is to assume the fault for the family's issues, bear your father's most noticeably terrible maltreatment, and handle outlandish obligations. In any case, as the narcissist's kid, you are externalized, not regarded as an individual with your own personality. Your narcissistic dad discloses to you what you think and believe and demands your consistence with his variant of "reality" regardless of how foolish, bogus, or hurtful.

One of the most troublesome and significant things you should accomplish for yourself as a survivor is to set up sound limits. Understanding what that implies and getting open to doing it can require some investment and practice for the offspring of a narcissist. The primary spot to begin is with the narcissist parent and conceivably other relatives.

Your Emotions are Real, and You Should not Ignore Them

As the offspring of a narcissist man, you have been deliberately prepared to disregard your emotions, even to dread and abhor them. Your sentiments are an immediate danger to your dad since they are probably going to strife with what he needs, accepts, and requests. In the narcissistic family, just the narcissist's sentiments matter, and every other person's must be sublimated or by and large squashed through scorn, disgrace, rage, and different types of assault.

Maybe the most significant activity for yourself toward mending is to reconnect with your emotions. They are there, and they generally have been. Give them access, hear them out, convey them with deference. In your sentiments, you will find yourself and your way through and out of the narcissist's "elective realities" world. Since you have been disregarded in multitudinous manners by your parent(s), you should explore through serious hurt and outrage. Most narcissistic dads always project their own insane intentions and feelings onto others. They criticize others or even blame them for their very own harsh conduct, so from the outset, you may not realize what you genuinely feel versus what you have been mentally conditioned to accept. As you figure out how to adjust to your sentiments, show restraint.

Make an effort not to pass judgment on yourself. Emotions are sentiments. They merit, and in the plan of things demand, acknowledgment and respect.

Try not to Feel Guilty

Especially if you are the Scapegoat in your family, you are probably going to accuse yourself consequently and feel blame for things outside your ability to control or obligation. Narcissistic dads are specialists at diverting and anticipating fault onto others. If they seethed at you and you defended yourself, you assaulted them. On the off chance that they punched you, you drove them to it. Perhaps the ideal approach to break your undesirable relational peculiarities is to quit blaming yourself for what was never your obligation or deficiency regardless.

Break the Pattern of Destructive Self-Abuse

Alongside not accusing yourself, odds are you have to stop examples of self-misuse. As somebody brought up in a narcissistic family, you are inclined to dangerous, self-rebuffing, and self-mitigating; however, harmful practices, for example, substance misuse and addictions, self-damage, and rush chasing. Your foolish conduct is a disguise of the narcissistic maltreatment you grew up with, which is something contrary to the narcissist's externalization of her agony. By taking part in such conduct, you keep on giving the narcissist control over you. You likewise fuel the passionate and physiological injury you have just persevered. Examples of compulsion and self-damage can be complicated to break, so look for help and backing from individuals who comprehend the elements of narcissism.

Try not to Hook up with Another Narcissist

To add further damage, numerous grown-up offspring of narcissistic fathers are defenseless against being brought into associations with narcissists past their group of inceptions, including accomplices, companions, and managers. It sucks, yet there is no disgrace in this: Repeating the past until we gain from it is the mind-body's method for mending. So, focus. Learn. Continue teaching yourself about narcissism. Build up a calibrated narcissist radar, or "nardar." If you get stumbled in undesirable connections, excuse yourself and proceed onward. Just around 6 percent of individuals have NPD. There is a lot of not narcissists out there, so get them!

Perceive the Disappointment you Feel

A great many people love their dad, regardless, and we stick to our requirement for adoration and approval from them. Sadly, your narcissistic father can't cherish you genuinely how we as a whole have the right to be adored inside our families, and so far as that is concerned is prepared to do close to momentary compassion. However, you may, at present, love that parent. Blended in with despondency and outrage, you may likewise feel for your father's NPD. It is also conceivable that you are numb to your dad or, too, utilized something like feel love any longer.

Whatever you feel, make an effort not to pass judgment on yourself for it. Respect your emotions and let them be your guide by the way you decide to interface with your family. Decide not to stay in touch with them if that feels like the most secure decision. Or on the other hand, work with firm limits and brought down desires. Narcissist fathers, except if they are genuine perverted people, are typically equipped for a fondness for their kids, at any rate now and again. Some might have the option to give in manners that you find sustaining or accommodating. With a sound portion of incredulity, take the great when it comes, as constrained as it might be.

Dispose of the Narcissistic Traits in You

Youngsters raised by a narcissistic dad are probably going to get up probably some narcissistic characteristics. Some become all-out narcissists themselves, however numerous only propagate a couple of practices that can be overwhelmed with care and practice. Investigate yourself. What triggers you? Which activity makes you remember your narcissist father? Is it true that you are brisk to outrage? Do you look for consideration or control through blame or control? Would you be able to be progressively delicate to other's sentiments and viewpoints?

The best vengeance is an actual existence well-lived. Work on care and harmony in your own life. You can't help how you were raised. However, you can work to control how you act now and how you bring up your youngsters

Notes:

_____
_____
_____
_____
_____
_____
_____
_____
_____
_____
_____
_____
_____
_____
_____
_____
_____
_____
_____
_____
_____
_____
_____
_____
_____
_____
_____

Narcissistic Fathers

Chapter 2: Complex Post-Traumatic Stress Disorder

If you grew up with a narcissistic father, be aware that your early days as a child have been filled with volatile unpredictability. You won't have encountered conventional love from your parental figure, and this will have hurt how you control your feelings and states of mind.

A narcissistic father with NPD that was not diagnosed will make you experience childhood in an upsetting home, which is a result of his unstable emotional episodes.

You will probably have grown up always trying to avoid your dad's unstable and unusual emotional episodes — their capacity to feel for you conventionally and clearly will have been inclined to abrupt and rough encounters.

Sometimes your dad could be so kind and adoring, yet you never can predict when his temperament would change. It could occur over any flimsy situation, like scouring your eyes excessively.

If you were brought up in this sort of condition, you are probably going to have issues unwinding and confiding in anyone around you. You won't have had the option to depend on your father, conventionally. Subsequently, your ability to unwind, to be unconstrained, to be inventive, and to play will most likely be undermined. Having awesome relationships will probably be troublesome.

This is where you develop c-PTSD; Complex Post-Traumatic Stress Disorder.

At the point when you have survived a youth that included these sorts of erratic and horrendous upheavals, especially if there was nobody accessible to help and relieve your problems with, at that point, it is likely for you to have developed this disorder.

Individuals who have survived undiagnosed awful encounters like these can go onto the build up a wide range of emotional and mental issues. I have a lot of understanding of working with individuals who are alluded to me on account of manifestations like:

- Tension and Anxiety

- Strange diseases

- Rest issues

- Lack of Focus

- Addictive practices

- Problems with Spouses

If such a person tries psychotherapy, it begins to turn out to be evident that the side effects they are showing are really sitting over a more seasoned issue.

It may become astonishing, but many individuals who live with these sorts of issues are with c-PTSD without acknowledging it.

In the situation where a child grew up with a narcissistic father who was inclined to abrupt and flighty brutal upheavals, or whose possess passionate needs occupied the entirety of the room, it tends to be difficult to pay attention to your own needs.

If no one else were there to care for you and love you unconditionally, at that point, you would battle to do this alone.

The awful upheavals of a narcissistic father which you have lived with for long will give you issues in areas like:

- Focus

- Profession

- Relationships

- Dejection and confinement

- Alcohol and medication issues

Kids who have been brought up in these sorts of situations can battle to proceed to do a wide range of things. In any case, it is conceivable to recoup and fix the harm done by your childhood.

However, it requires some serious energy and duty.

Some portion of what makes it so troublesome is figuring out how to confide in your therapist. Being fortunate, you will arrive at a point in your treatment where you can get through that questioning hindrance and find that trust is conceivable.

Now you will easily see that the hidden issues throughout your life have been brought about by the injuries of your initial involvement in your narcissistic father. What's more, if you can get to this point with your specialist, you can go onto doing it with others as well. Try not to let your life stay detained from before, don't stay a prisoner to your narcissistic and damaging guardians.

What Is C-PTSD?

This term is firmly identified with PTSD (Post-Traumatic Stress Disorder).

As an anxiety disorder, a person's PTSD can suffer from it after he/she encounters a horrendous accident. However, a specialist may analyze complex PTSD if an individual has encountered drawn out or rehashed injury over a long period (years or months).

Manifestations of PTSD like dread, severe tension, having dreams or flashbacks, or doubt can emerge after an awful scene, for example, a fender bender, a quake, or rape. Indications may incorporate bad dreams, shirking of circumstances that bring back the injury, increased reactivity to upgrades, uneasiness, or discouraged disposition. Additionally, usual signs are passionate about separation or undesirable thinking.

The side effects of c-PTSD can be a lot severe and outrageous than the usual post-traumatic disorder.

A specialist has to analyze complex PTSD when an individual has encountered an injury that is still occurring. Most times, this injury includes long haul physical, enthusiastic, or sexual maltreatment.

In light of its complex nature, **Social Experts** may discover another condition in its place. They might probably recognize BPD, which is Borderline Personality Disorder.

Major Symptoms Associated with c-PTSD:

Low Self-esteem: Complex PTSD can make an individual view themselves adversely and feel vulnerable, guilty, or embarrassed. They frequently believe themselves to be not quite the same as others.

***Changes in convictions and perspective*:** People with Complex personality disorder may carry around a contrary perspective on the world and the individuals in it or lose confidence in recently held convictions.

Troubles with Controlling Emotions: These conditions can make individuals lose power over their feelings. They may encounter serious displeasure or trouble or have considerations of suicide.

***Problems with spouses*:** With c-PTSD, relationships frequently end in disaster because of challenges trusting and connecting, and due to bad self-esteem. An individual with either condition may create undesirable connections since they are what the individual has known before.

Separation from the injury: You can detach yourself from traumatic experience by feeling disengaged from emotions. A few people totally overlook the injury showing no emotions to it.

Wrong Focus: People with c-PTSD are fond of focusing their mind on the narcissistic father, the association with the abuser, or seeking retribution for the maltreatment.

Different indications include: remembering the injury through bad dreams; maintaining a strategic distance situations that remind you of the past; tipsiness or sickness when recollecting the trauma; hyperarousal (This is a persistent condition of high alarm the conviction that the world is a risky spot); second-guessing yourself and people around you; difficulty in sleeping at night; being frightened by loud commotions.

Manifestations of complex PTSD can fluctuate, and they may change after some time. Individuals with the disorder may likewise encounter side effects that are not recorded previously.

Individuals that are down with complex PTSD can display certain practices trying to deal with their side effects. Instances of such practices include:

- Substance abuse; drugs or liquor

- Always trying to accommodate people to avoid horrendous circumstances

- Showing emotions over minor reactions

- Hurting oneself

These practices can form as an approach to manage or disregard the traumatic injury and emotional torment. Frequently, an individual develops these symptoms throughout the traumatic experience. When the injury is never again continuous, an individual may start to mend and limit the way they depend on it. Or on the other hand, the practices may continue and even compound after a while. Family members and relatives of people with c-PTSD ought to know that these sorts of practices reveal some ways of dealing with stress and endeavors to deal with feelings.

Overcoming C-PTSD

To recoup from complex PTSD, an individual can look for treatment and figure out how to supplant these practices with ones that are increasingly positive and productive.

Treatment choices for complex PTSD incorporate psychotherapy, EMDR, which stands for (Eye Movement Desensitization and Reprocessing, and medicine):

EMDR (Eye Movement Desensitization and Reprocessing)

This treatment is an intuitive psychotherapy strategy used to soothe mental pressure. It is an excellent treatment for all forms of trauma and PTSD. After planning and practice, your expert therapist will request that the individual review the horrible events. The therapist will move his finger from one corner to another, and the individual will pursue the development with their eyes.

At the point when successful, this procedure makes the patient oblivious to the trauma. This way, they can, in the long run, review the memory without having a solid unfavorable response to it. EMDR is still under study due to opposing arguments based on the fact that the accurate component by which it works is yet to be fully understood.

Psychotherapy

This can be done for a single person or a small gathering to treat complex PTSD. It may happen on a balanced premise or in a gathering setting.

At first, treatment will concentrate on balancing out the individual so they can address their sentiments, including doubt and negative perspectives, improve their associations with others, and manage flashbacks and uneasiness. The significant treatments utilized are:

Cognitive Behavioral Therapy (CBT) is a kind of psychotherapeutic treatment that assists people with realizing the musings and sentiments that affects the way they act and make decisions. CBT is ordinarily used to heal different forms of disorder, including fears, depression, and uneasiness.

DBT (Dialectical Behavior Therapy) focuses on showing individuals how to live at the time, adapt strongly to pressure, control feelings, and improve associations with spouses. It is a form of Cognitive Behavioral Therapy.

Notes:

Narcissistic Fathers

Chapter 3: Making Boundaries

It takes a few years for most grown-up kids to understand that a narcissistic father raised them. Some of the reason behind that is supposing that you grew up with a narcissistic dad, you were persuaded that the source of the problem is You;

You are so flawed, didn't invest in the relationship with your father; you are a bad egg, and that you weren't fit to earn such unrestricted love.

Nonetheless, when you understand that it was really your parent's business to give that affection, to support you instead of cutting you down and that your narcissistic father was unequipped for giving those things, it very well may be liberating.

There is generally a grieving period after you understand this reality since all the hurt and torment that your narcissistic father caused upon all of you your life at long last has a protected spot to come spilling out. In the long run, however, you can start the mending procedure, and you can start discovering ways in which you can cherish yourself, take good care of yourself, and make it a need to stay within a circle of individuals who can adore you without strings attached.

However, what should you do when your narcissistic dad refuses to let go of his influence in your life?

One of the most difficult to-acknowledge parts of growing up with a narcissistic dad is that significantly after you've grown up, they will, in general, need to remain engaged with your life. Keep in mind: As an addict, they love to control, and all the time, they have to infantilize their association with you so they can keep the dad-kid progressive system set up for as long as they want.

That may happen in the form of unreasonable telephone calls; intruding in each enormous or little choice you make; creating solid rules about the individuals you decide to bring into your life; proceeding to condemn you in profoundly personal and destructive ways; and maybe, in any event, controlling you with cash, emotional blackmail, or pay off.

Generally, narcissistic dads have a ton of issues "cutting the line" with their kids, which can leave their grown-up youngsters feeling belittled, hurt, and defenseless long after they have left home.

Anyway, what are your alternatives here?

Some children have chosen to separate from their narcissistic, dangerous dad; it is the best course for their psychological well-being, particularly if their conduct keeps on hurting them all the time. The choice to cut off the association with your lethal dad is an individual choice undoubtedly, and one everybody needs to make dependent on their particular conditions.

Practically, those who have settled on that decision did as such after profound thoughtfulness, and for the most part, in the wake of making a decent attempt to make the relationship as sound as would be prudent. At long last understanding that things were probably not going to change and that expelling such father figure from our life was the best choice for everybody included. It's a long, debilitating, passionate procedure.

In any case, a few children haven't gotten to that spot or are as yet investigating our choices. So, what would we be able to do to keep on having an association with a narcissistic dad and still keep up our emotional well-being?

Set Boundaries and Be Strict

Tell your narcissistic dad what is and isn't alright as far as their conduct or requests is. Instruct him to what degree he can keep on being engaged with your life. Tell him how frequently he can call, visit, or communicate with you.

It's about you are getting the chance to choose for once with kind of relationship you want to keep with your parents, and the opportunity to place your own solace and psychological well-being in the front line.

What happens if you become straightforward about your limits? The truth is, he won't care for it. You should be set up for that. Limits are his adversary since it implies that he may have lost a bit of their essential command over you. Your father will push back, and you need to relentless yourself and stand firm.

This is the place you're going to need to rehearse all that self-esteem and recall how awesome and fabulous you are. Your limits are for you to set, and you should set them for your mental soundness. And afterward, it isn't your concern whether your dad can manage them. That is dependent upon him to live with. You aren't a terrible girl or child since you have made your needs known. That is actually what sound individuals do, and great on you for taking a shot at that.

If your narcissistic dad returns at you hard, it is useful to have a few reactions close by to manage the circumstance. You can even record them or type them into your telephone, so you don't lose your considerations when you get overpowered. These announcements can extend from a humane, however unfaltering reaction like, "I apologize for what this might do to you. I love you. However, this is what I want, and, significantly, you acknowledge them," to an all the more emphatic reaction like, "I have been straightforward about what I want. I don't anticipate examining anything with you." Your distance may differ, yet it's imperative to be calm and direct.

Here and there, you should work on avowing those limits consistently until your narcissistic dad gets it. Also, now and again, your most solid option will be just to leave the relationship, either incidentally or for good. This is really important because you are important. Your wife and kids matter as well, and they are looking out for you. If a relationship is harmful to your general prosperity, at that point, it may be an ideal opportunity to separate yourself from it.

You should have an encouraging group of people set up as you explore these troublesome, difficult changes you are making in your association with your dad. A stable wife or companion who truly gets you and adores you without strings can be refreshing. Also, you can look for a decent specialist or advisor. We all merit empathetic expert assistance as we chip away at advancing our lives.

Above all, recollect this: You didn't request to be naturally introduced to a home with a narcissistic dad in charge. In any case, you get an opportunity consistently to start once more; to connect with all the magnificence and brightness that is inside you, that is always there. You have the right to feel needed, regarded, and safe. It is your life; the rules are yours to determine. Don't forget that. You are stronger than you can imagine.

Five Ways to Set Up Boundaries

It's anything but a simple procedure to set boundaries between you and your toxic father. It needs time to review occasions and change them to a newfound reality. It involves gigantic vitality to reconstruct the negative words and aggressive activities of the narcissist. It requires inspiration to finish the procedure until another degree of wellbeing is accomplished. In any case, since this procedure is done, what new limits can prevent the grown-up from falling go into old propensities?

Plan Ahead

Before visiting or addressing your dad, the grown-up ought to recollect his father is a narcissist. It may be useful to survey a portion of their glaring qualities so desires can be all the more properly set. When an individual realizes a lion is a lion, they ought not to anticipate a sheep. Contemplating the discussion before it starts enables the grown-up to arrangement appropriately. Choose to set sensible desires.

Advise Yourself of your Dad's Nature

It is best to imagine that the discussion will shift its focus to the narcissist. Though the underlying inquiry might be about the grown-up, it rapidly changes to the narcissist every time. Grown-ups ought to expect this and keep answers quick and painless to abstain from parting with vital information that he can use against you. They will always utilize the extra information against the grown-up sometime in the not too distant future. Choose not to give out data.

Decline to be cross-examined

A frequent strategy of narcissists is to overpower others into a condition of elevated nervousness, so they are less ready to think correctly. Grown-ups fall into this snare effectively as their narcissistic dad prepped them through extraordinary cross-examination as a youngster. This is about power and control for the narcissist. When your dad starts, you should hinder their relaxing. At that point, answer the inquiry they wish the narcissist posed rather than the one that was asked and promptly tails it with a commendation: this incapacitates and diverts most narcissists.

Reject boisterous attacks

Hauling insults is another narcissistic strategy. They obnoxiously ambush anybody seen as a threat. The grown-up might get themselves an objective for a forceful, inactive forceful, or blame ridden remark. This is about the examination that keeps up the narcissist's unrivaled status. On the off chance that the grown-up gets cautious, the narcissist father has won. Or maybe, the grown-up ought to overlook the remark or state "that is not fitting" and again offer a diverting commendation. This keeps the grown-up from acting like the narcissist. Choose not to be a narcissist by being defensive against his negative remarks.

Don't Allow yourself to be Victimized

If all things are not working for the narcissistic father, he turns into the injured individual as a method for lay the blame on the grown-up till he surrenders. There "it is my fault" routine is tweaked to coordinate the shortcoming and weaknesses of every grown-up youngster. It is continuously powerful else, and the narcissist would stop this conduct. It helps if the grown-up kid sees this grouping like that of a two-year-old fit. The more positive or negative consideration that the two-year-old gets, the more the presentation is rehashed. The key here for the grown-up is to overlook the narcissistic father's lead altogether. Much the same as a two-year-old, it will take a few endeavors before the new reality sets in and isn't rehashed. Reject any type of controls.

After a timeframe, these new limits will become propensities for the grown-up, and the effect of your narcissist father will be significantly decreased. Best of all, even though the relationship appears to be shallow, it is more severe than it seems.

Narcissistic Fathers

Notes:

Narcissistic Fathers

Chapter 4: When Your Narcissistic Dad Is Sick and Aging

Numerous grown-up offspring of narcissistic dads are winding up in the sandwich age. Studies uncover that most grown-ups are all the while supporting their youngsters and grandkids while additionally giving help to maturing guardians.

It's an unpleasant time for a lot of people. But, consider the possibility that that maturing guardian is your narcissistic dad, and thusly you don't have a compelling, passionate association with him. Maybe there has been abused as a child and a long-lasting absence of love or closeness. Perhaps you have a shallow relationship and discussion just about the climate or everyday subjects. Presently your parent has arrived at the age where elderly consideration is required. What do you do?

The lack of resources being extended in numerous ways is unquestionably a noteworthy issue. In any case, there is an extra strain for grown-up offspring of narcissistic dads. At the point when you grew up with a narcissist, the parental sound chain of command is slanted. The youngster is required to be there to cater to his father and ignore his own needs. At the point when that parent turns out to be older, the desire turns out to be progressively serious. The adult child's conscience starts bothering. All of a sudden, you begin to guilt-trip, clear disconnectedness and upsetting beloved recollections cause an inner fight. All things remain the same in narcissistic homes — the examples rehash. You wind up in one more grown-up section of life. What would be the best next step?

I've conversed with grown-up offspring of narcissistic guardians on all parts of the bargains. Some have taken their fathers back in, and some have kept in touch, some had endured because they didn't have sentiments when the parent passed on, and some are amidst it at present. The limited resources and care makes the whole situation almost impossible to bear. I accept the appropriate responses that exist in every person and family situation and depends solely on the adult child's phase of recuperation.

Inside the narcissistic family, you will probably discover a lack of association or disavowal with different individuals, kin, and so on., some may have grasped the idea of narcissism and most who have not. In this way, you are left with you and your personal wars.

Blame isn't your best friend. However, I do accept there are two significant interesting points. One is your value ideology, and the other is your phase of recuperation. Some may respond with, "Our dad needs us!" "We are ghastly individuals on the off chance that we don't react at this moment," or, "My dad has consistently been requesting, and here it is once more." We can securely set aside some effort for our thought and be okay with that freedom. It might be forlorn, yet it's a piece of this developing season.

Such harmful guardians raised some grown-up youngsters that they couldn't associate with them or give them love. This is likewise a great way to preserve yourself. Be that as it may, it is a personal choice and ought to be made after recuperation steps are followed and grasped. Every one of us comprehends what is directly for us when we set aside the effort to work the recuperation. We can't pass judgment on another's away. I know numerous individuals who needed to settle on a choice to totally isolate from their group of the starting point and in light of current circumstances.

In the midst of these personal wars, realize that you truly are not the only one — link with others to know how they overcome this challenging soul-searching phase.

Why you should not feel regretful about not caring

In reality, do we owe our narcissistic dads anything, in their weak moments or dying days? Is it true that we are committed to thinking about them? Is it okay to now accept them back into our lives because they are now sickly and old? In a situation where we have made the 'No Contact' pledge, what should we do?

Numerous societies and faith systems advise that youngsters should think about their folks in their mature age, similarly as their folks thought about them in their youth. Hypothetically, it is a great rule. However, in a scenario in which your father is a narcissist and all through his life, he made your life miserable, should you just follow the rule?

Remember that the typical narcissist does not change because of age. Even though some do change, which is what some would like to believe, in most cases, studies show that narcissists behave much worse as they get older. Indeed, even the beginning of Alzheimer's does little to relax them, truth be told, it can also make them increasingly merciless.

First and foremost, you didn't request to be conceived; nobody asked for it nor thought about it. It was a decision made by our parents. What's more, provided that you are still breathing, your dad more likely than not invested in your upbringing: nourishment, garments, housing, and tutoring. However, the careless narcissistic dad simply performed his essential obligations and ensures their teenager feels indebted and regretful for the basic things he provided, even in a harsh condition. The immersing narcissistic dad goes far beyond ensuring their youngster feels obliged and remorseful for everything their folks demanded accomplishing, regardless of whether it was needed.

In both instances, growing up with a narcissistic man makes you feel obliged and liable. Be that as it may, you shouldn't! It wasn't your thought nor decision to be conceived.

The reason why you should not care is doubled if your father is an interminable narcissist. This implies that he had made your youth a horrendous experience: your teenagers' life ghastliness and your twenties a minefield of hopelessness. Nevertheless, presently, he anticipates that you should invite him into your extra room until their last day.

Don't feel compelled to. The narcissistic dad relinquished any case to mind in their mature age when he has done any of the following:

- Sexually abused. If they did it to you, they could do it to your children.

- Physically molested you by beating, slapping, or tying you up.

- Obnoxiously maltreated you for a considerable length of time.

- Refusing to support you financially

- Gave a valiant effort to isolate you, estrange you from your companion.

- Gave a valiant effort to distance your kids from you, urging your children to disregard you.

For each situation, your dad relinquished any case to senior consideration when they did all of the above. They endeavored to slaughter any adoration you had for them. In every way that really matters, you are dead to them. What's more, a dead kid can't enjoy an older parent. Your matured guardians can and will move for themselves, in one way or another, someway similarly as they would if you had really died before them. Try not to let their miserable or helpless show trick you!

Caring For your Narcissistic Father Yourself

However, if you eventually decide that you want to take care of them, remember that this can be a great choice and considerably more depleting than thinking about the non-narcissistic father. You should cautiously consider your choices here, pondering your very own emotional well-being. On the off chance that you have just settled on the decision to think about your parent yourself, guarantee that you take regular breaks and get as a lot of outside help as you can to hold your confidence, feeling of self, and point of view.

If you are inside the narcissistic condition for a long time without outside breaks, you will think that its a lot harder to hold your very own psychological well-being. Have a decent encouraging group of people, and you may likewise wish to connect consistently with a specialist.

Disregard His Gaslighting

This is the conduct you are now acquainted with, and if not, at that point, you should know about it. A narcissist will frequently attempt to make you feel as if you are losing your brain or that you are preposterous, and this conduct has gotten known as 'gaslighting.' This conduct could form with the beginning of dementia if they have not recently displayed gaslighting behavior.

It may be that they reveal to you that you recall a circumstance mistakenly, or attempting to disclose to you that your recognitions are not right, or continually demanding they are the person in question and you are accomplishing something incorrectly. They will make you question yourself and are endeavors at control. This can make it staggeringly hard to talk about what they need care, or you may feel constrained into thinking about them.

Disregard self-fault and different controls

Narcissism can incorporate touchiness, they attack you, alongside an admonishing. This can be extraordinarily hard to explore while you are attempting to think about your parents. It tends to be simple for you to slip into feeling like an admonished kid once more.

For instance, you place a feast before your parent that you took care of getting ready, and your parent gets cross, saying 'I don't need you to utilize that plate, I TOLD you this current.' It's critical to keep yourself in the now, advising yourself that you are a grown-up and in charge of your own life. Try to avoid panicking and understand this is just a control strategy to enable the narcissist to feel prevalent or their very own projection sentiments of deficiency. You can offer to change the plate in this model, or state that you will recollect this for next time.

Utilizing a Caregiver

Narcissists will once in a while look for care for themselves and will likely loathe any type of maturing. On the off chance that you choose that thinking about your narcissistic parent will be, or as of now is excessive, there is no disgrace in giving over the consideration of your parent to a consideration supplier and in any event, separating yourself. Here and there, we need to protect our mental soundness and well-being from dangerous connections.

Discussing your parents requiring care isn't something that will work out in the right way for the narcissist, so it very well may be a great idea to find support from a specialist in anticipation of this. The exchange is probably going to wind up with you feeling remorseful. You should be stable and disclose what will occur, guaranteeing that you hold your limits and adhere to your arrangement. If you have a supportive group of people or different individuals from the family to help with this, get them included.

Getting outer assist will spare you from a great deal of despair. A utilized consideration specialist will have the option to treat your parents with respect and care, yet also have the opportunity to deal with their character. Your parent might be a troublesome individual to help, yet a decent career will have the option to help them regardless of this. It is a lot simpler for an individual without your enthusiastic connections to have the opportunity to manage the narcissistic parent.

How Caregivers can adapt To Narcissistic Men

An old narcissist is probably not going to change their conduct. Analysts concur that NPD is so hard to treat, even in youthful, physically sound individuals.

Analysts concede that thinking about a narcissist isn't simple and is probably going to provoke one profoundly of their being. In any case, these are three things guardians can do to adapt to narcissistic men.

Do as much as you can to get a break, keep up a public activity, or something to that effect and take part in exercises that you appreciate and that restore you. Look for expert assistance from an advisor or therapist to assist you with figuring out your emotions and learn separation.

Set individual points of confinement on how much misuse you are eager to take and adhere to them regardless. It's likewise essential to recall that an association with a narcissist is, viably, a single direction road. Those with NPD propensities are so up to speed in themselves that they have a restricted capacity to cherish others, comprehend their points of view, or worth their feelings. Genuinely tolerating this reality will assist you with recognizing your job as a defender and supplier for somebody who cannot respond with sentiments of affection, gratefulness, or even resistance.

Know Your Limits: Take obligation regarding your enthusiastic state. Keep in mind; you can't control a narcissist. You can just control yourself.

What a narcissist does not want is for their parental figure's needs (or anybody's needs, truly) to supplant their own. Parental figures are generally benevolent people, and those with NPD regularly utilize this to further their potential benefit. Yet, you should recollect that you are significant, as well. Your well-being and satisfaction matter. Rolling out essential improvements to your circumstance will expect you to keep your best interests in mind for once. It will be troublesome, yet this is absolutely not something to feel remorseful about; it is a need.

The Difference between Narcissism and Dementia

It very well may be hard to see dementia in an individual who is narcissistic, particularly in the beginning periods of subjective decrease. You may battle to recognize genuine memory issues and gaslighting conduct, and they may utilize gaslighting to manage it. In beginning periods of dementia, the narcissist will blame others for their

259

absent-mindedness. Anyway, this could likewise be an ordinary event in maturing. Things being what they are, how might you tell if a narcissistic parent is creating dementia?

As their psychological capacities decay with dementia, it will turn out to be especially evident, you should be perceptive in their practices to spot changes. As they will keep on accusing others, however, will be bound to pull back from others to spare their sense of self, instead of blossom with the consideration.

When serious intellectual decrease is in progress with the narcissist, this is where they might be in danger of suicide; a narcissist is bound to finish, as opposed to utilizing it as a device for consideration. At the point when they are never again ready to take care of themselves, narcissists shut down and may once in a while act like a non-narcissist individual. Relatives may stick to this with trust; however, the movement of dementia is excessively cutting-edge. Outrage upheavals will be regular just as jumpy daydreams. The narcissist is so persuading even at this phase; they can attract others into their hallucinating state.

If your parent has generally been non-narcissistic and appears to have abruptly built up some of these qualities, this may likewise be demonstrative of dementia.

Notes:

_____
_____
_____
_____
_____
_____
_____
_____
_____
_____
_____
_____
_____
_____
_____
_____
_____
_____
_____
_____
_____
_____
_____
_____
_____
_____

Narcissistic Fathers

Chapter 5: Self-Healing

If a narcissistic dad raised you, there are ways to achieve self-healing and reduce some side effects of the harm done. For years, your dad has endeavored to obstruct your freedom, while you wrestle against their profound want to frame a free personality. Now, as a grown-up, you may encounter decreased confidence and an inescapable yet unwarranted feeling of shame. This is always found in households that are headed by a narcissistic father. He uses all forms of manipulations like trying to separate siblings with triangulation, thereby forcing them into unfortunate partnerships with him. Children are treated differently is such households, with one being the perfect person and the other being flawed. At face esteem, the estrangement of a parent who is experiencing psychological maladjustment may appear to be pointlessly brutal. Nonetheless, adult offspring who don't end the narcissistic burn through direct activity are the ones well on the way to propagate the inconvenient examples in their very own grown-up connections.

If you had a narcissistic father and you feel prepared to relinquish the undeserved passionate weight that you convey from your adolescence, here are a couple of quick advice for putting the past behind you:

A decent initial step is recognizing the misfortune you encountered through the nonattendance of what ought to have been a loving and steady parent. Losing a father is troublesome at any age, yet when the misfortune happens from the get-go throughout everyday life, it tends to be particularly tragic to process. Permit yourself and your brother/sister a grieving period. Start working through the lamenting procedure — enable yourself to lament the parent you never had. Recognize that you've never figured out how to manage sentiments appropriately, and start to begin working through these emotions.

You ought to help your sibling remember that nobody was to be faulted for the issue. Little teens frequently choose to take up the guilt for a family's brokenness. Now that you are an adult, the time has come to relinquish any dishonestly placed blame.

Recognize the unique quality and awesomeness of in you and your siblings. Look beyond the unfortunate practices that were the aftereffect of being brought up in such an irregular situation. Utilize the positive improvements inside the new relationship as an approach to get the compassion and unqualified respect that your father was not able to give you as kids.

Recuperating from such horrendous youthful days is an overwhelming process. This is because your emotional needs have been neglected for such a long time may make the thought of recuperation apparently unthinkable. It's most certainly not. Work toward cherishing that little kid inside you in the manners your Narcissistic father could not imagine.

Quit trusting that your father will change; once again, narcissists do not change.

Do not forget to tell yourself consistently that you have to love and cater for yourself – attending to yourself is very significant. Keep in mind that you are an essential and unique person.

Quit hurting yourself or abhorring yourself. You also deserve adoration and commitment because you're an extraordinary individual.

Quit fearing your father – you are a grown-up, you've endured a lot of abuse already, and you have to recover your life.

Eradicate personal fears. Dispose of that sentiment of not fitting in or having a place. Your Narcissistic dad instilled such a mindset, and it must go.

Discover and associate with other mishandled kids. Look for a specialist who has an involvement with treating issues this way.

You're most likely still scared of stumbling into difficulty because of how your Narcissistic father treated you. You're a grown-up now, and you should not live to please anybody yet yourself. Discharge a portion of that outrage. Crush a few plates. Shout. Hit a cushion. Do anything to let your resentment of being manhandled by your narcissistic dad, go far from you.

Figure out how to be self-sufficient. Begin by settling on little choices for yourself, and understand that you are responsible for your very own life.

You are more than commendable. Regardless of what your Narcissistic dad let you know, you are more than excellent.

Stay away from guilt-tripping. It is your closest companion and most exceedingly terrible foe. This is a really tough fight considering the number of sentiments to battle against, yet you should. At the point when that blame is chewing ceaselessly at you, speak against it. You don't have to feel remorseful if you choose not to keep in contact with your Narcissistic dad it might be to your benefit.

Recall that your needs are significant. Try not to be hesitant to make them known and request what you need.

Isolating yourself from the kind of codependency that is regular from Narcissistic dads may appear to be overwhelming. Indeed, they were genuinely or physically harsh, yet as the maxim goes, "your dad is as yet your dad." But, now that you have grown, you must make one of these two choices to set yourself free from the entanglement of your father:

Complete Estrangement – This implies that, till your dad kicks the bucket, you are getting in touch with him for whatever reason.

Estimated Contact – This implies that your contact with your dad is limited with strict rules to follow. For instance:

Make extremely clear limits. Try not to reward your dad for stepping over the boundaries. Be straightforward and rigorous. If they appear unannounced, clarify that you are too occupied to even think about coming to meet them.

Protect your kids from their Narcissistic Grandfather. They should not be presented to their poisonous actions. Instead of clarifying that you would prefer not to hear their recommendation, reverberate, and mirror whatever your dad says. Go ahead with your plans all the same.

When your dad is getting older, employ a caregiver, or contact them with the help of others. You should not enable them to depend upon only you because of their old age.

Notes:

_____

_____

_____

_____

_____

_____

_____

_____

_____

_____

_____

_____

_____

_____

_____

_____

_____

_____

_____

_____

_____

_____

_____

_____

_____

_____

_____

_____

_____

_____

Narcissistic Fathers

CONCLUSION

We have examined extensively what it means to live and deal with a Narcissistic Father. Healing from Family Narcissistic Abuses can't be separated from accepting that the narcissistic parent can't be changed because he simply doesn't want. His behavior (or in the worst case Narcissistic Disorder), while imposing the idea of perfection, also remove from his mind any purpose of psychological treatments: "If I am perfect, why should I need help? Maybe they need a counselor."

Psychotherapy can help the children of narcissistic fathers to understand and elaborate on what has happened within their family.

In the safe and welcoming lounge of the therapist, you can experience all the pain for the ideal parent that you would have desired and that life has denied. You would recover the relationship with the brothers that the narcissistic parent wanted to make enemies. You would regain confidence and create a new alliance with the succubus parent, who is also a victim, and give yourself a unique chance to still enjoy your family.

It is necessary to allow ourselves to express anger, sadness, and pain for long time repressed or denied: there are no right or bad emotions; there are only emotions that can help us to free ourselves from the past and to meet our future. A future in which healthy love is always possible: just give yourself the chance to recognize it and feel deeply. We have examined the reasons responsible for the narcissistic behavior of your father.

Healing is near and healing is yours.

I hope you had useful information by reading Narcissistic Fathers. Please let me know your sincere thoughts by leaving a short review on Amazon. Thank you.

Printed in Great Britain
by Amazon